Dolores Curran

Family Prayer

The complete guide for praying families

Twenty-Third Publications
P.O. Box 180
West Mystic, CT 06388

I dedicate this book
to our godchildren—
Annette
Cheryl
Jimmy
Michael
Monica
and
Sam

Cover design by Ed Curley

Cover photo by Patrick Mooney

Library of Congress Catalog Card Number 78-64453

ISBN 0-89622-087-7

Contents

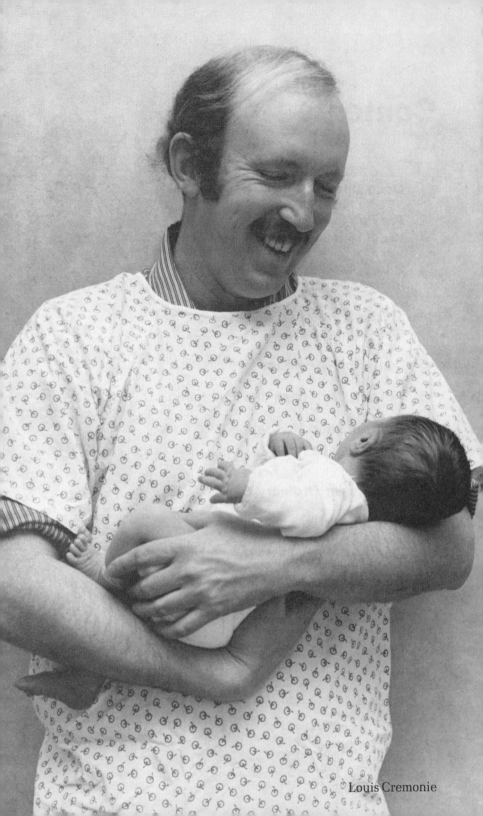

Louis Cremonie

1
Once Upon A Church Prayers

The Our Father—Parent Style

Our Father, who art in heaven
Where it's quieter than it is at home
Thy kingdom come, Thy will be done
But meanwhile Thy parents need help!
Give us this day our ration of wisdom
And forgive us our weaknesses
As we forgive those of our children.
Lead us not into vexation
But deliver us from despair
For thine are the babies,
The teenagers and the parents,
Now and forever. Amen.

"Do memorized prayers have any value?" parents often ask me. "I don't see the point in teaching them to our children if they don't understand what they're saying."

Yes, memorized prayers do have value, as long as they are not the only prayers offered a child. The primary value of memorizing any material, whether it's prayers with incomprehensible words, history dates, or math tables, is that the material is there when the person grows up to understand and need it. Maybe children won't understand all the words in a prayer now, but later on, when they are in need of a quick reassuring prayer, they will reach for it and understand it. And it will be there because they learned it.

I try to caution parents not to teach the more complex prayers too soon, but rather to begin with the simple understandable ones.

The first prayer I remember learning as a child was, "Angel of God." I can still conjure up my very own angel who sat at the foot of my bed and watched over me once the lights went out. It is an immensely reassuring prayer when you are little and frightened of being alone or of things that go bump in the night.

Since I've become a parent and experienced my children's little fears, I've come to realize even more the value of a personal guardian angel and the prayer that goes with it. I also contrast it with the line in the classic children's prayer, "If I should die before I wake." What a horrible prayer to say with children at bedtime. I would never teach my children a prayer that instilled fear. For a toddler's first prayer, I don't think we can surpass "Angel of God."

Angel of God

**Angel of God, my guardian dear
To whom God's love commits me here,
Ever this day, be at my side,
To light and guard, to rule and guide. Amen.**

It was always an occasion in my childhood family when the youngest mastered the Sign of the Cross.

Since there were seven of us close together, the young learner had a great deal of help, probably too much at times, but I remember all of us watching and holding our breath when the toddler finally put the correct words with the correct motions at family mealtime. And that's how we've taught the familiar basic prayers to our own children, by saying them as grace until they have mastered them. This gives them practice, a bit of glory, and affirmation by loved ones.

Sign of the Cross

In the name of the Father, and of the Son, and of the Holy Spirit. Amen.

We like to follow this with the "Glory Be," which, incidentally, makes a fine prayer to end the family meal. Simply bow your heads together and say,

> **Glory be to the Father**
> **And to the Son**
> **And to the Holy Spirit**
> **As it was in the beginning,**
> **Is now,**
> **And ever shall be,**
> **World without end. Amen.**

My mother never taught religion but she was wise in teaching us how to pray. She began with the small simple prayers, interspersing spontaneous prayers, and saved the harder more abstract ones until we were a bit older.

We were a great family for making visits to church. She taught us this little verse when we were very young. When she was dying and we were all around her bed, we said it again to her. It brought a smile to her face and tears to ours.

**Whenever I go past a church
I stop and make a visit.
So when I'm carried there some day,
Our Lord won't ask, "Who is it?"**

We taught our children the Our Father and the Hail Mary in bits and pieces so that they could better understand and assimilate each phrase at a time. At mealtime, we began with, "Our Father, who art in Heaven," and talked a little about that word, "art." Since most children will run into poetic and archaic language in prayers only, it's important to let them know that words like "art, thou, and thy" are retained because of tradition, much like the " 'twas" in " 'Twas the night before Christmas." Otherwise, as they grow up they will tend to equate outdated language with outdated prayer.

At mealtime or bedtime try teaching the Our Father in several segments rather than one large gulp. Here's how we did it.

(Monday dinner) *"Our Father, who art in heaven . . . .* let's all say it together a few times. Good, Tomorrow night we'll see if we can remember it and if we do, we'll add the next line."

(Tuesday) "Who remembers the first line to the Our Father? Good, Let's hear you say it. That was fine, Tim. Oh, you remember it too, Sue? Good. Anybody else? Okay, the next sentence is *Hallowed be Thy name.* Let's say it together. Good. Does anyone know which two words are said exactly the way they were hundreds of years ago? Right. *Hallowed* and *thy.* Want to guess what they mean?"

(Wednesday) "Let's say the first two lines together: *Our Father, who art in heaven, Hallowed be Thy name.* Good. Let's try it again. Okay, now we add *Thy kingdom come, thy will be done."* And so on.

This is a better approach than simply having a child memorize a lot of words as he does with a television commercial. It also shows him that the prayer is important enough for the family to talk about it, not just learn it. Go through it in the above way until the family has learned it comfortably.

The Our Father

Our Father, who art in heaven,
hallowed be thy name;
Thy kingdom come,
Thy will be done on earth
as it is in heaven.
Give us this day our daily bread
And forgive us our trespasses
As we forgive those who trespass against us;
And lead us not into temptation,
but deliver us from evil.
For thine is the kingdom
And the power
And the glory
For ever and ever. Amen.

Once your family has mastered the Our Father, go into the Hail Mary. You are familiar with the pattern of learning so it is a natural progression. In both prayers, there are some phrases and ideas that are too abstract for little minds: "thy will be done," and "fruit of thy womb," etc. Don't avoid them but don't dwell on them, either. Give the children the words so that, as they grow to understand, they can put the meaning to the words.

You might explain to a four-year-old, for example, that "thy will be done" means that whatever God wants, you will do, or that "fruit of the womb" means baby. Expect the child to ask, "Then how come we don't say it that way?" Be ready with your response, "Because it is a prayer that is hundreds of years old and it is nice to keep the language that way if you're big enough to be able to say it." The inference to maturity usually insures quick learning.

Hail Mary

Hail, Mary, full of grace,
The Lord is with thee.
Blessed art thou among women
And blessed is the fruit of thy womb, Jesus.
Holy Mary, mother of God,
Pray for us sinners,
Now and at the hour of our death. Amen.

Another word here about language. Many parishes and teachers are using modern language in the standard prayers. There's nothing wrong with that. We attended a rosary service recently with relatives from many parts of the country and the responses were evenly divided between "The Lord is with thee" and "The Lord is with you." If you prefer to teach your children this modern version of the old prayer, here it is:

Our Father, who is in heaven
Hallowed be your name.
Your kingdom come, your will be done
On earth as it is in heaven.
Give us this day our daily bread
And forgive us our trespasses
As we forgive those of others.
Lead us not into temptation
But deliver us from evil
For yours is the kingdom,
the power, and the glory,
Now and forever. Amen.

And the modern version of the Hail Mary:

Hail, Mary, full of grace
The Lord is with you.
Blessed are you among women
And blessed is the fruit of your womb, Jesus.
Holy Mary, mother of God,
Pray for us sinners,
Now and at the hour of our death. Amen.

Although we much prefer spontaneous grace to the familiar, "Bless us, Oh, Lord," we feel it's important to teach our children the traditional Catholic grace. There are many times that it is used in large groups and in other homes and then they need the words.

Bless us, Oh Lord, and these your gifts
which we are about to receive from your
bounty, through Christ, our Lord. Amen.

The grace after meals is not said as often as it might be in families. It just might be the right closing ritual between dessert and the rush to turn on television.

We give you thanks, Almighty God,
for these and all your blessings;
you live and reign forever and ever. Amen.

It's easy to teach our children to pray to God and to Jesus because they are "people" to them. It's much harder to teach them to pray to the Holy Spirit. I've found the best way with small children is not teach about the dove and tongues of fire, which, because of their concrete level of understanding, only confuses them more, but to teach that the Holy Spirit is that feeling of love that emanates from God and Jesus, much like the feeling of love that emanates from one another when the family is intimate. To build up a devotion to the Holy Spirit, it is necessary that a child hear about Him and this traditional prayer said daily by the family helps build a familiarity.

Come, Oh Holy Spirit, and fill the hearts
of your faithful. Kindle in them the fire of your love.
Send forth your Spirit and they shall be created
And you shall renew the face of the earth.
Oh God, who has taught the hearts of the
faithful by the light of the Holy Spirit,
grant that in the same Spirit,

**we may be always true
and ever rejoice in his consolation.
Through Christ, our Lord. Amen.**

Once upon a church, we taught the Act of Contrition at age seven so that the child could recite it at his or her first confession. We know now that the child didn't understand the words and that for many adults, prayers learned as children became frozen at that level their entire lifetime. In most parishes today, private confession is put off until age 10 or so when the child is more aware of the meaning of sin, contrition, and forgiveness. Various forms are used in confession today and it is possible that a Catholic would never "need" the Act of Contrition. But it is a traditional prayer that is both beautiful and meaningful. We have taught it to our children at age 10 and we use it during our family reconciliation rituals.

Act of Contrition

**Oh my God, I am heartily sorry
for having offended you,
and I detest all my sins
because of your just punishments,
but most of all because they
offend you, my God,
who are all good and
deserving of all love.
I firmly resolve,
with the help of your grace,
to sin no more and to avoid
the occasions of sin. Amen.**

I've put off the Apostles' Creed as long as I could. There's a real problem in teaching this to our children today that we didn't have. When we learned it, the Creed at Mass was in Latin so we didn't confuse the two. But today's children hear the Creed at Mass every

Sunday and then are expected to learn an Apostles' Creed just different enough to cause a good deal of confusion. Yet, they need to know the Creed for the rosary and their own personal use. We don't insist that they learn both but one of our children did. The other two use the Creed from Mass when we say the rosary.

I believe in God, the Father Almighty,
Creator of heaven and earth,
and in Jesus Christ, his only Son,
our Lord, who was conceived by the Holy Spirit,
born of the Virgin Mary,
suffered under Pontius Pilate,
was crucified, died, and was buried.
He descended into hell;
the third day he arose again from the dead.
He ascended into heaven,
sits at the right hand of God,
the Father Almighty;
from thence he shall come to judge
the living and the dead.
I believe in the Holy Spirit,
the Holy Catholic Church,
the communion of saints,
the forgiveness of sins,
the resurrection of the body,
and life everlasting. Amen.

Every family has little traditions and rituals. We have a whole series of them when we travel. One is to say a rosary every day in the early morning in the car. Often, this coincides with the rising of the sun. Everyone is still a bit subdued and a little hungry. It's a fine time to put our day on the road in God's hands.

Many parents report that their children dislike the rosary because they find it meaningless and repetitious. (Yet, many of these same children have grown up to embrace forms of meditation which are based on meaningless repetition!) We have found that if we emphasize the mysteries of the rosary rather than the prayers, our children respond well.

When they were young, we began by telling a little story explaining each mystery. Now that they are older (10, 13, 17), they give a sentence or two explanation of each mystery. In the car, nobody is rushed. There are no phones, television set or other distractions. Maybe that's why the rosary works so much better for us in the car than anywhere else. Anyway, I encourage other parents to try it when they travel, even if it's only a one day trip. The family can take turns saying the decades and rotate the joyful, sorrowful, and glorious mysteries on different days. Here are the mysteries and the stories we told that accompanied them:

Joyful Mysteries

First Joyful Mystery—The Annunciation: "When Mary was just a young girl, an angel came and said to her, 'Hail Mary, full of grace, the Lord is with Thee.' He asked her if she would be willing to become the mother of Jesus and Mary said yes. We call it the Annunciation because the Angel *announced* that she was chosen to be the mother of Jesus."

Second Joyful Mystery—The Visitation: "When Mary was pregnant, she visited her cousin, Elizabeth, who was much older than she but was also pregnant with Jesus' cousin, John the Baptist. When Mary and Elizabeth hugged each other, their babies leaped inside as if they were greeting each other. Later on, it was John the Baptist who prepared the way for Jesus by telling people he was coming."

Third Joyful Mystery—The Nativity: "This is Christmas, the birth of the infant Jesus. You know the story well, but let's recall it for a moment. Remember that Joseph and Mary had to go to Bethlehem to register for the census and while they were there, Jesus was born. There was no room at the inn so he was born in the stable. Later he was visited by shepherds and wise men."

Fourth Joyful Mystery—The Presentation: "This is a little like our baptism today. Each Jewish baby was taken to the temple and 'presented' to the rabbi there. It was during this time that the old man, Simeon, who had been promised by God that he wouldn't die until he saw the saviour of his people, saw Jesus and said, 'Now I am ready to die. I have seen our Saviour.' "

Fifth Joyful Mystery—Jesus in the Temple: "When Mary, Joseph and Jesus had gone to Jerusalem with a large group of people for a special day, the women walked back together and so did the men. At suppertime, when families gathered together again, Jesus wasn't there. Mary had thought he was with Joseph and he thought Jesus was with the women. They had to walk the long way back and they must have been worried that something happened to Jesus. But they found him in the temple teaching some of the teachers. And he was only 13! When they asked him why he hadn't come with them, Jesus told them he had to be about his Father's business. This was one of the first signs Mary and Joseph had that Jesus would be leaving them someday to do God's work."

Sorrowful Mysteries

First Sorrowful Mystery—The Agony in the Garden: "After the Last Supper, Jesus told his friends, the Apostles, that he wanted to go to the garden to pray. They went with him and he went in a little farther to pray alone. When he came back, they were asleep and that disappointed him because he knew he wouldn't be with them much longer. After awhile, the soldiers, led by Judas, came and took him away to be tried and killed."

Second Sorrowful Mystery—The Scourging: "Even though Jesus hadn't hurt anyone or been tried by a court of law yet, the soldiers stripped his clothes away and beat him."

Third Sorrowful Mystery—Crowning with Thorns: "The soldiers were making fun of Jesus. Because he said he was a king, they made a crown for him out of thorns and stuck it on his head until his skin bled. Then they pretended to bow before him as their king."

Fourth Sorrowful Mystery—Carrying of the Cross: "Jesus had to carry his own cross through town and up the hill to Calvary. On the way, he fell three times, met his mother, and said a silent goodbye to her, and was made fun of by the people in the street. Finally, he made it to Calvary where he was nailed to the cross."

Fifth Sorrowful Mystery—The Crucifixion: "Jesus died on the cross. It took three hours of great pain and sadness. He was crucified between two thieves. One asked his forgiveness and Jesus said to him, 'This day you shall be with me in heaven.' When he died, his body was taken down and laid in Mary's arms."

Glorious Mysteries

First Glorious Mystery—The Resurrection: "The morning that Jesus rose from the dead on what we call Easter, some of the women were coming to his tomb to anoint his body. When they got there, the stone was rolled back and an angel told them Jesus was gone. They ran into town to tell the men who were hiding. There was great rejoicing when they heard. Thomas, one of the followers, didn't believe and Jesus came to them in the upper room and asked Thomas to put his hands on his wounds so he could believe it really was Jesus."

Second Glorious Mystery—The Ascension: "After awhile on earth, Jesus arranged to meet his disciples on a mountaintop and told them to continue his work. They remembered when he had told them that in a little while they would not see him but then in another while they would. It was his way of saying goodbye to them in this life but telling them he would see them in heaven. Then he rose into the heavens and disappeared into the clouds."

Third Glorious Mystery—The Descent of the Holy Spirit: "After Jesus ascended into heaven, the Apostles were gathered together preaching when the Holy Spirit descended upon them. Suddenly they were filled with great love and knowledge. Every person listening to them could understand them, regardless of the language the listener spoke. In our Church today, we call this Pentecost Sunday. Some people call it the birthday of our Church because it gave the Apostles the spirit, love, and wisdom to go out and preach. Also the courage."

Fourth Glorious Mystery—The Assumption: "We do not know how this happened but we do know that Mary died and went to heaven. We can just imagine what a glorious reunion there was there between her and her son. She was *assumed* or taken up into heaven. That's why we call it the Assumption."

Fifth Glorious Mystery—The Crowning of Mary as Queen of Heaven: "Mary, as the mother of Jesus, reigns as queen in heaven. Remember, that when Jesus was dying, he gave his mother to all of us. In heaven, she remains our mother and our queen. That is why we pray the rosary to her and speak to her in times of love and need."

As our children get older, they want more mature prayers. "Angel of God" seems too babyish to them (although they may whisper it in the dark) and some of the others are too mechanical. The family should constantly add prayers so their repertoire becomes a growing rather than a stagnant tradition. An old favorite of mine, "The Morning Offering," seems foreign to many children and adults today. I offer it here to your family as a good way to face each day.

**Oh Jesus, through the Immaculate Heart of Mary,
I offer you my prayers, works, joys,
and sufferings of this day in union with the
Holy Sacrifice of the Mass throughout the world.
Amen.**

I got through many a test, argument, and date with the aid of The Memorare. This beautiful prayer shouldn't be allowed to be forgotten. Say it in May with your family during grace or include it in your Mary rituals.

The Memorare

**Remember, O most gracious Virgin Mary,
that never was it known that anyone who fled to
 your protection,
implored your help, or sought your intercession
 was left unaided.
Inspired by this confidence, we fly unto you,
O Virgin of virgins, our Mother!
To you we come, before you we stand, sinful and
 sorrowful.
Oh, Mother of the Word Incarnate, despise not our
 petitions,
but in your mercy hear and answer us. Amen.**

In a survey taken not long ago, Catholics said, more than anything else, that they missed Benediction, the ritual that ended many of our evening novenas, Stations, and missions in the pre-Vatican II Church. I wonder if it was the mysticism of the grandeur and incense that surrounded it or if it was because it combined ritual and language. At that time, of course, the Mass and even the Solemn Forty Hours were conducted in Latin so we weren't certain what was being said. But we always knew what was taking place during Benediction.

Benediction ended with the Divine Praises. I am including them here, not because I think families should hold Benediction at home, but because these might be useful in family celebrations and parents might be able to preserve them in their children by so using them.

The Divine Praises

Blessed be God!
Blessed be his Holy Name.
Blessed be Jesus Christ, true God and true Man.
Blessed be the name of Jesus.
Blessed be His most Sacred Heart.
Blessed be His most Precious Blood.
Blessed be Jesus in the most holy Sacrament of the Altar.
Blessed be the Holy Spirit, the Paraclete.
Blessed be the great Mother of God, Mary Most Holy.
Blessed be her Holy and Immaculate Conception.
Blessed be her Glorious Assumption.
Blessed be the name of Mary, Virgin and Mother.
Blessed be St. Joseph, her most chaste spouse.
Blessed be God in His angels and in His saints.

Finally, here is my favorite prayer, The Prayer of St. Francis of Assisi. It so perfectly states the apostolate of the Christian and in such beautiful language, that I see it as a highly valuable prayer to the family, especially to young people. It has also been put to music under the title of "Lord, Make Me a Channel of Your Peace," a beautiful song to use in family paraliturgies. We use it during our Advent, Lent and Reconciliation rituals.

Prayer of St. Francis of Assisi

**Lord, make me an instrument of Thy peace.
Where there is hatred, let me sow love.
Where there is injury, pardon;
Where there is doubt, faith;
Where there is despair, hope;
Where there is darkness, light;
and where there is sadness, joy.
Oh, Divine Master,
grant that I may not so much seek
to be consoled as to console;
to be understood, as to understand;
to be loved, as to love.
For it is in giving that we receive,
it is in pardoning that we are pardoned,
and it is in dying that we are born to eternal life.
Amen.**

For those favorite prayers of your family, that I have failed to put in this chapter, here are a few blank pages. By putting them in, you are personalizing your family collection of prayers and keeping them all together in one place.

Favorite Prayers
of Our Family

Favorite Prayers
of Our Family

Favorite Prayers of Our Family

Louis Cremonie

2
Praying In The Family—Not Just Saying Prayers

A Spontaneous Prayer

Hi again, God. How are you today? I am fine. One question I wonder about. How come you don't fall out of heaven? Well, that's all I've got to say, I guess. Gotta go now. Bye.

—— Mark

Prayer by a nine year old

Sometimes after I've given a talk on prayer and celebration in the family, a listener will object to the idea of spontaneous or natural prayer because it detracts from memorized prayers. I call this the either-or mentality. Why can't we have both? We need the memorized prayer to reach for in a hurry or when our creative well is dryer than usual. We need spontaneous prayer when a memorized prayer just doesn't say what we want to say to God.

I think it's sad when a child hasn't learned his or her prayers but I think it's far sadder when a grownup can't pray spontaneously. One thing is obvious, though, the earlier the child is exposed to spontaneous prayer, the more comfortable the child will be with it.

When the child is very young and you are tucking him into bed, say the "Angel of God" with him and then add a homemade prayer of your own like this:

"And thank you, God, for Timmy and for this good day. Amen."
or
"Take care of us tonight, Jesus, and keep us well. Amen."
or
"Help us to love one another and you tomorrow, Jesus. Amen."
or the familiar
"God bless Grandma, Grandpa, my friends, etc."

Don't repeat the same thing every night but encourage the child to add his or her own words. Be prepared for some strange prayers, like, "And, Jesus, please hit Danny for me because he took my Big Wheel." Spontaneous prayer is just that. If we land heavily on our children for praying in their own words to God, they will soon be praying in our words, and that defeats the idea.

Family grace is by far the most effective time to teach spontaneity in prayer. The dinner table is the only time many families get together in our hectic culture. If parents use it for intimacy with one another and God, it implants the idea that God is an integral part of family life.

Parents serve as models in teaching family grace. Get into the habit of saying something like this before meals:

Oh, God, we thank you for this food,
for the rain today which we need,
for Tommy's field trip to the museum,
and for each other. Amen.

That's enough for young children. Keep it simple, understandable, and short. If there are two parents, take turns saying grace. The whole family responds with a simple "Amen."

When the oldest child is able, invite him or her to say a homemade grace. You will be surprised at how comfortable and capable he is at it because he's heard and watched you do it. His first grace is likely to be something like this:

Jesus, thanks for the chicken and the potatoes and the milk and the peaches and grandma and today.
Amen.

Sometimes you may have to cut him off because his newfound verbal skills don't often command such rapt attention and he will go on endlessly. Do it gently by saying—when he has to pause for breath—"and thank you, Jesus, for such a good grace. Amen."

If the child is timid or if you are initiating original grace with older children, adopt the technique of having one of the parents say the grace and each of the children adding a prayer of thanks, like this:

Parent: "We thank you, God, for this family, for our home, for all our various works today, and for this good food."
Second Parent: "Thanks for helping me get all my work done today."
Oldest child: "Thanks for letting me catch the bus which I almost missed."
Second child: "Thank you, Jesus, for getting my paper put up on the bulletin board."
. . . . and so on, through all the children.

As children get up into third grade or older, they can take on the family grace all by themselves. Many families tell me that they like to alternate among them in order from oldest to youngest because this gives the grace a freshness at each meal.

A word here about song. If your family is uncomfortable praying together in the beginning, try singing the great Amen or one of the familiar hymns from Mass as a grace. Add a thanks for the food, either before or after the song. This is an especially effective way of getting into natural prayer in a family where there is no tradition of it and there are pre-teens or teens.

Someone once observed that the songs of today are our youth's poetry. I think the same is true of prayer. Teenagers are often more comfortable singing their prayers than saying them.

If the family is really uncomfortable about spontaneous prayer—uptight, in the words of today's children—try the old memorized, "Bless us, Oh Lord," and add a phrase or two of thanks. Gradually increase this until you can drop the security of the memorized prayer in favor of original prayer. Don't rush it. It may take some time, particularly if your children are older and used to a five-second grace instead of a two-minute one. But keep in mind that you are taking the effort to furnish a balanced meal. Why not a balanced family—parents, children, and God?

Mealtime prayer also offers us the opportunity to touch. In many families today members do not touch one another in any loving way. (They may hit or fight.) They do not hug, kiss, or throw their arms about the shoulders, even after an absence from one another. Yet, there is a great hunger for this in both parents and children. If your family is disadvantaged in this way, try joining hands for family grace. It's a simple yet loving gesture that is non-threatening to even the most closed-off member of the family.

I once worked with a family that did everything "right," from scrupulous attendance at Mass, church meetings, and religious education to keeping a chart on the children's morning and night prayers but this family had no sense of familialness, no intimacy, no touching, no openness to one another.

The parents dutifully attended a lecture I gave in their parish about family prayer and celebration, and they came up afterward to ask me if it was too late to instill a sense of celebration and openness in their family's spiritual and emotional life. I suggested that they continue with their spiritual regimen (because that is how I viewed it) but that they add one ritual. Before dinner, they were to join hands and sing The Great Amen.

They reported back that it was awkward for the family at first, but before long they were able to drop the formal grace and get into spontaneous prayer and eventually some other family rituals. What struck me was the mother's comment, "You know, I think what we all like most is the holding of hands . . ." In that family, just the holding of hands was both a gift from and a prayer to God.

From Mealtime to the Rest of the Time . . . .

Once the family is comfortable with open prayer before meals, try expanding it to other times during the day. Again, you as parent, are model. How naturally you invoke God, Jesus, the Holy Spirit, Mary, and patron saints during the day is apt to be how your children will invoke them also. If you save prayer for those rare occasions when it's quiet and you have 15 minutes to get down on your knees privately, so will your children. If you are in the car and glimpse a view of the mountains and breathe a spontaneous, "Thanks, God, for such beautiful mountains," so will your child come to pair creation and thanksgiving. If an ambulance goes by and you say aloud, "Dear God, bless the person in that ambulance. Please keep that person from too much pain," your listening child will pair God's saving grace with your concern for others.

A natural time for natural prayer is the moment of waking the child in the morning. Say something like this:

Good morning, Katie. Time to get up. Thanks, Lord, for my little Katie and for a brand new day.

(A touch on the shoulders here can be a gift to the child as well as a bonus for Mom.)

Contrast the above with the more usual shout on your way to the kitchen, "Get up, Pete! It's 7 o'clock."

Other natural times for spontaneous prayer are those moments during the day which call for a quick word of praise, of thanks, or of need. Again—and forgive me if I stress this too much—the example of a parent comfortably reaching for a quick prayer is the best method of instilling it in the whole family.

When the child comes home from school crushed because he was the last one chosen in the recess ballgame, the parent who is comfortable with God can say, "That's really too bad, Joe, but God must have a reason," and then take the child's hand in hers and say, "We know someone has to be last in everything, Jesus, and please help us to learn to be last sometimes. Still, it hurts to be last and help Joe's hurt not to be so much."

This little prayer may not seem to be much on the surface, even schmaltzy, but let's look at its values. First, it brings God in on concrete matters in daily life. Secondly, it implants the idea in the child's mind that somebody has to be last. Third, it affords an opportunity for touching. And fourth, it tells the child that the parent understands and is on his side.

Joe will probably eat a banana or two and go out and find someone to play with, and the parent will have an hour or so before the next child comes home, say this one a junior-high daughter who has just made the gymnastics team. It's just as important to talk with God together in moments of triumph. The parent can calm the leaping, excited girl and then say something like this:

"Ginny, it's super that you made the team. I'm so glad. Let's say a prayer of thanks together ... thank you, God, for Ginny and for helping her make the team. Let her have a good year and help her win a few, okay?"

Again, this little prayer or one like it can be powerful in the parent/child/God relationship. If parents only understood the value of it in terms of the three-way interaction, they would use it more. It gives the parent an excuse to tell the child how pleased she or he is (or how disappointed) and this is often hard for parents to do. It gives the child a chance to hear a parent share concern and pleasure over him or her alone. It gives both a sense of security in recognizing God as a member of the family.

Once the family gets accustomed to little moments of spontaneous prayer in the daily routine, it's a natural step to pray around a campfire, at the seashore, before a big event, and after a disappointment. I will be talking much more about the use of spontaneous prayer in seasonal rituals. That's why I wanted to put this chapter up-front.

Before I finish with this type of prayer, let me point out a few pitfalls. If parents are aware of them before adopting them, it might save their first tender experiments with natural prayer from failure in their homes.

1. Don't put on a false face or voice while praying. My son calls it a "church face." All of us tend to change our voice and our language when we pray. We get more solemn, in some cases more pretentious and artificial. Try to work that out of your prayer life. The more naturally you pray, the more naturally God becomes real to your family.

2. Don't always assume a praying posture. If a prayer is to be natural, you should be able to say it while sitting in a lounge chair on the patio, while taking a walk, or while lying down. In a fine film, "What Do You Think?" (Geneva Pub. Co.), Dr. David Elkind interviews several young children, asking them, among other religious questions, "What is prayer?" Many of them replied that it was hands and knees. To children, it is often so. They see the externals of praying as the prayer itself.

3. Don't wait until the children are around to pray

naturally. Children are very quick to recognize when something is done for the sake of the children. Breathe a prayer aloud during the day even when nobody else is around. Pray spontaneously with your spouse. This will make prayer more natural to you and you will unintentionally pass on this comfort to your children.

4. Don't overdo it. I'd rather see parents who didn't pray spontaneously at all than those who pray too much. Occasionally after a retreat or encounter weekend, parents will come back and turn the home into a mini-monastery, praying upon rising, upon washing, upon eating, upon going to school, and so on. The best word here is gradual. Learn to love prayer as a part of your family life by allowing it to develop on its own.

5. Don't force children or your spouse to pray openly. Spontaneous prayer has to be just that. ... spontaneous. It isn't spontaneous if we say a prayer and then stare at someone and wait for him to come up with one. It isn't spontaneous if we say tersely, "I don't care what's on television, we're going to pray openly and lovingly RIGHT NOW." It isn't spontaneous if it's assigned. It isn't spontaneous if it's memorized. It defeats its purpose if the child—especially the teenage child—feels pressured to pray because the others are praying. To avoid this, don't go around the table or from parent on down but invite those who want to participate to do so.

It is well to remember that we are novices in this area of natural or spontaneous prayer. We grew up in a Church of ritualized prayer, one in which we weren't expected to or invited to participate outside of the routine responses. Spontaneous prayer, however, is natural in many faiths. And our people today are showing a great desire for it. The startling popularity of prayer groups and charismatic prayer attests to this. Why not begin it in the family and allow it to grow in its own way? It can add a spiritual dimension to family life that has been missing for years, maybe even for generations.

3
Ritual, Tradition, and Celebration in Today's Family

A Family Prayer to Mary

Come into our home, Oh most loving mother Mary,
and make yourself a part of our family.
Hear us when we are lonely.
Comfort us when we are sad.
Heal us when we are torn.
Celebrate with us, enjoy with us.
Share with us those moments of intimacy
that transform a family from the mundane to the
  unique.
Honored Mother, invite your Son, Jesus
into our hearts and our midst.
Let us reflect the light of His love
in all that we do here at home,
and let the rays of His love
extend from our family to His family everywhere.
  Amen.

I mentioned earlier that today's family has a great hunger for ritual. Paradoxically, we see parents denying any such hunger. Why? Probably because they are uncomfortable with the idea of celebrating God openly and naturally with their children. What we see in this kind of family is the eventual seeking of ritual and prayer outside of the family or parish circle.

Young Catholics are strongly attracted by Jesus groups and campus prayer people. It has been estimated that 30% of all young people attracted to the Unification Church, better known as the Moonies, are Catholic. Most of these young Catholics explain their attraction to the Moonies in terms of absence of real prayer and spirituality in their own faith, particularly within their families.

How can the Catholic family replace the rituals and traditions lost during the past decade or two with rituals meaningful to today's children? Most of today's families do not respond to rituals of an earlier age in our Church: family rosary, novenas, and litanies. Most do respond to open prayer, song, and communal celebration. Our task as parents is to learn how to change, to adapt, to furnish new religious experiences in our homes so that our children will not have to seek them elsewhere.

I had the privilege of serving on the Writing Committee on Family for the 1976 Call to Action consultation initiated and funded by the American bishops. We waited expectantly for parents to let us know what they wanted from their Church. Right near the top, they asked for more support for family values and included in this category a desire for "more home worship activities like the home Mass." They were asking for rituals which would give a family the same sense of religiosity that the rosary did in another era but the closest they could come in describing such rituals was the home Mass.

One of my greatest pleasures in working with Christian parents comes from helping them instill a sense of ritual and celebration in a formerly sterile family religious climate. Although many approach it with trepidation and sometimes apology in their families, they soon discover that their children love it. To a child, once is a tradition. Many a parent, after implementing a nameday celebration or family meditation for the first time, will hear his child say to another, "Oh, we *always* do that in our family."

Following are my Ten Commandments for Family Ritual and Celebration:

Ten Commandments for Family Ritual and Celebration

I. Let the Ritual Serve the Family, Not the Family Serve the Ritual.

One of the problems with the old Advent Wreath ritual (the only one Catholic families of the past could identify as a home ritual), was that the prayers and format were so stylized that they prohibited flexibility and spontaneity. Many families who tried that ritual and found it wanting gave up on family prayer and went back to private prayer. The language was archaic and the words meaningless to young children. The order of the ritual was set down word for word and, like many other early rituals in the home, resembled more a "mini-Mass" than a real family religious celebration.

We must not become enslaved to any rituals. Repeat that to yourself several times. If, in one of my rituals that follow, you feel the words are alien to your family or that another order or combination or prayer would be more effective, by all means change them. God gave you your family, your common sense and your faith. Combine them in the most nourishing way possible.

If a particular ritual does not emerge around your table as perfectly as it does in print, don't worry about it. Above all, don't consider yourself or the ritual a failure. The celebration, not you, may be at fault. There is nothing holy or enshrined about these rituals. They are merely words. You are the ones who put the spirit into them.

I've written before about our first family Passover-Holy Thursday meal, I took it all upon myself, used a linen tablecloth, candles, grapejuice, and the works. Our children were very young. I handed Jim, my husband, the stylized prayers and we began. It bombed. The kids didn't understand the words. They spilled the grapejuice and blew candle wax onto my beautiful cloth. I was dismayed and by the end of the meal felt a real failure. But everyone else thought the ritual was great. "Can we do it again next year, Mom?" they asked eagerly. That experience told me that I was trying to turn our informal family celebration into one worthy of a cathedral. Once I stopped trying to do that, our family rituals became more open, more relaxed, and more spiritual.

II. Initiate at Least One Annual Religious Ritual in Your Family.

Tradition is what family is all about. So important are traditions that some marriages flounder on whether the gifts should be opened Christmas Eve, as it was always done in the wife's family, or on Christmas morning, as it was done in the husband's family. There are daily traditions, of course, such as how the family seats itself around the table or how it observes Saturday morning, but the usual family traditions surround special days or religious holidays.

Family therapists delve deeply into the sense of tradition in the families they are trying to help. The most solid intimate families have many traditions: they celebrate each person's birthday in a special manner, they go to the mountains or seashore every Fourth of July, they invite the same people to First Communions, and so on.

I try to encourage Christian families to develop one religious tradition that is uniquely theirs. The possibilities are endless. Many are mentioned in the second half of this chapter.

One very popular tradition is the annual family home Mass. We like to have ours in May, partly because it began with our eldest child's First Communion that month, partly because May is one of the quieter months in the family calendar, and partly because it is an excellent way to bring Mary more intimately into our lives.

Families who do have an annual home Mass report that their children more willingly participate in the Sunday parish Mass after they have experienced the intimate Mass where they can actually see the consecration and pray aloud together.

III. Retain or Rediscover the Ethnic Religious Traditions That are your legacy.

When I was speaking in Texas once, Bishop Patrick Flores of San Antonio heard me stress the value of religious tradition in the family and he said to me later in his soft Spanish inflection, "As you were talking, I couldn't help but think about my people. They have such beautiful religious traditions but they feel they have to shed them in order to become truly American. Please encourage them to keep them in their families and in their homes."

Sadly, that's what happened in too many American families, not just among Hispanic peoples but among the Italians, Basques, Irish, Polish, and Germans who migrated here. There seemed to be a race to shed old country traditions that gave a sense of identity to the peoples, the parish, and the families.

The Italians with their beautiful St. Joseph's day custom of setting up food altars in their homes and inviting people to come and sample and leave an offering for the poor; the Irish with the blessing of the fields and the wakes; the Polish with their Holy Saturday food baskets to be blessed for Easter; the Mexicans with the Posada at Christmastime—these and hundreds of ethnic customs too good to let disappear—need to reappear in the family.

Check your roots and re-instill a few of the more meaningful religious traditions in your home. Ask the older people about old customs. Visit the ethnic parishes in your area. If you are the typical American family, your roots consist of ties to several cultures. Then adopt what you like from each culture.

IV. Give Your Family Rituals Time, Space, and Planning.

Good family celebrations don't happen; they are planned. Look ahead on the calendar and schedule your Lenten activities, your Pentecost brunch, or your summer meditation. Too many parents adopt the "we'll-get-around-to-it-sometime" mentality when considering family prayer and ritual. We know we won't get around to it but rather we must get to it ourselves if we are to initiate a sense of spirituality in the family before our children leave home and seek it elsewhere.

Sit together as a family and decide what rituals you would like to try this year. Perhaps you will want only three: a home Mass, an Advent and a Lenten ritual. Or perhaps you will be like our family which has the following: Epiphany, Ash Wednesday, weekly Lenten Stations of the Cross, family reconciliation, Holy Thursday, Passover dinner, Pentecost, namedays, wedding anniversary, Mother's Day, Father's Day, May home Mass, Mary ritual, Back-to-school ritual, All Saints, Thanksgiving, daily Advent, and various Christmas rituals.

Believe me, we never intended to have so many, but once the children got into ritual and celebration, they liked it as an intimate family bonding and looked forward to these times of sharing.

Few of our rituals are long, maybe 20 minutes at the most. But they require planning. Someone has to be in charge—a parent at first, but a child does nicely once he gets old enough and familiar with the season.

Some families like to celebrate in the living room, others around the family table, still others outside if the weather cooperates. Find your family's special time and place. The greatest difficulty in scheduling time comes from gathering today's family together all at once—a remarkable feat in families where the babysitter has to leave before the paperboy gets home or where family life becomes a series of notes on the refrigerator.

We find the time directly after evening dinner or Sunday afternoon the best for our family celebrations but you might prefer bedtime, before dinner, or Saturdays. Whatever you choose, do not try to work it in before an important television program. It's defeating to condense a celebration meant to relax and bind the family, into 12 minutes because The Muppets are on at 7:30.

V. Get a Book or Two on Family Prayer and Ritual.

If you own this book, you already have one. If not, get one for yourself or ask your parish to supply a variety of aids. You can't be expected to know prayers and rituals by heart, particularly if you didn't have a history of them in your own childhood family.

Remember that ideas beget ideas. Perhaps while reading some of these prayers, you will be moved to write some of your own for your own family. Dip into the Christian family magazines like *Marriage, Liguorian, St. Anthony Messenger,* and *Sign* for ideas. Ask your diocesan religious education office for my filmstrip, "Family Celebrations for Religious Education" (23rd Publications). It was designed for people like you. Ask for a workshop or class from your parish director of religious education on family ritual and celebration. He or she will be delighted that you care and want help.

VI. Share the Responsibility For the Ritual Among All Family Members.

Ritual and celebration should not be Mom's job but everyone's privilege. If one parent, usually the mother, takes ownership of it, she finds herself in the position of having to beg, defend, and cajole other family members into participating. Distribute responsibilities early. Even the youngest child can be made responsible for drawing a picture or choosing a song. Others can take charge of prayers, centerpiece and readings. During Advent, let each member take turns being responsible for the daily ritual. Encourage children to originate ideas for new rituals and occasions.

VII. Strive for a Blend of the Traditional and the New, the Memorized and the Spontaneous, the Reverent and the Informal in Your Celebrations.

Many Catholic families mistakenly believe there's nothing between the family rosary and the charismatic prayer group. We can best teach our children and ourselves a respect for other people's faith forms by exposing them to them. Begin your paraliturgies with a comfortable old prayer like The Memorare, continue with a spontaneous prayer to Mary. Have an old hymn like "Holy God, We Praise Thy Name," along with a new one like "It's a Brand New Day." Read from an adult bible and from a children's bible. Pray a traditional litany and then write one of your own.

In other words, keep the best of the traditional but don't be bound by it. Pass it on to your children. It's astonishing how many parents complain about their children's lack of familiarity with the old hymns and prayers without accepting their own family responsibility in furnishing them for them. The Church didn't drop the rosary, families did. We can't blame Sister for not teaching the morning offering or the importance of making visits to church if our children never hear us pray or see us make a visit.

VIII. Open Your Family Celebrations to a Wider Family.

A religious Sister once asked me if we ever invited Sisters from the parish to be part of our family rituals. "No," I replied. "They probably get enough of that in their work."

She corrected that impression at once. "We rarely get invited into families to be part of a celebration—only when we're there to furnish it. I would love to be invited as a guest to one of your Ash Wednesday rituals."

Since that time we have invited not only Sisters but people whose families live far away, shut-ins, clergy, widows and widowers, single adults, and family friends. When I work with families in learning to celebrate, I encourage them to open the family circle to others. The very essence of celebration is expansion—expanding beyond ourselves, beyond our own family, beyond our Christian horizons.

IX. Overcome Awkwardness and Embarrassment by Celebrating First With those Who are Comfortable With It.

If you are one of those families who find it hard to pray or sing aloud together, to hold hands, or to meditate together because you have never done it that way, then ask a celebrating family if you can join them for an advent or Lenten ritual so that you can see how it is done. Or ask your parish director of religious education or school principal for some demonstration celebrations or group rituals. Some parishes begin by having a family Advent Wreath ceremony the afternoon of the first Sunday in Advent for all the families in the parish. They then take the ceremony and spirit of it home with them to replicate during Advent.

If you have teens, it is a bit harder to get celebration started. Don't force them. Invite them to help with the music. Usually they are quite good at that. Let the younger children lead you into the prayers and sense of celebration. Their sense of embarrassment isn't yet developed and their refreshing candor and participation can make the rest of the family comfortable.

If you have a spouse who doesn't want to be involved, ask him if he will join you but do not give him an active role in it until he is comfortable with it. Ask one of the children to do the readings, another to do the prayers, and so on. If your spouse refuses to have any part of a spiritual ritual at home, go ahead and have one anyway. Don't deny the rest of the family the experience simply because their father is uptight. If the children ask why Dad isn't present, tell them you aren't really sure why he doesn't want to be part of it but defer their question to him. Let him respond to his children why he doesn't want to celebrate God with them. For too long, Mom has apologized for Dad in our Church. In order to allow Dad to grow up in his faith, we must make him responsible for his own religious leadership in the family.

X. Help Other Families Learn to Celebrate God Openly and Lovingly.

Faith and celebration are meant to be shared, not preserved. Once your family has tasted religious tradition and celebration in the home, it will want more. You will find your spiritual growth is natural and rewarding but there's a tendency to nurture it for your own sake. Once you feel you have established a comfortable degree of celebration in your family, offer to go on the parish liturgy committee and suggest some ideas to help other families to learn to pray and ritualize together. Work at making the Mass more participatory. Offer to become a demonstrating family for parish family workshops. Foster a parents' discussion group. In other words, take the blessings you have experienced from your family rituals and pass them on. That's the way of the Good News.

4
Through the Year In Prayer and Celebration

The Times of Our Lives

**"For everything there is a season,
And a time for everything under heaven."
Lord, let us make time for you, and
A time for a new year, a time for spring
A time for Lent, and a time for Easter,
A time for summer and for school to start
A time for Thanksgiving and a time for snow.
Oh, Lord, let us take time to celebrate You
In these times of our lives together.**

New Year's Day

Hymn: "It's a Brand New Day" (substitute year), "Alleluia," or your choice.
Spontaneous prayers of thanks for the old year.
Sharing of family spiritual resolutions.
Scripture: Either Genesis, the creation story, or— because this is the feast of the Holy Family—read Colossians 3: 12-17, 20.
Drawing: Each person draws a scene of the best family time or experience in the old year. Show and explain.
Final song: "Let There Be Peace on Earth," or your choice.

Presidents' Day (February)

Song: "America the Beautiful"
Sketch: Each member takes a hero and tells a bit about his or her life. (If parents take lesser knowns, children can "be" Washington, Lincoln, Columbus, etc.)
Draw: Together a large mural with butcher paper and felt-tip pens depicting blessings of God upon our country.
Song: "God Bless America."

(For Ash Wednesday, see chapter on Lent, Holy Week, and Easter.)

St. Patrick's Day

(This celebration can be done around a meal with corned beef and cabbage or Irish stew.)
Song: Favorite Irish song.
Tell the story of St. Patrick's life from any saints book. (This is a good time to get one if you don't have one. See bibliography in back.) Pass out large shamrocks of paper and draw symbols of the Church, the family, and the Irish. Post them.

Prayer from the Breastplate of St. Patrick:

Christ shield me this day:
Christ with me, Christ before me,
Christ behind me, Christ above me,
Christ beneath me, Christ above me,
Christ on my right, Christ on my left,
Christ when I lie down, Christ when I arise,
Christ in the heart of every person who speaks to me,
Christ in the eye that sees me,
Christ in the ear that hears me.
Closing song: Medley of Irish tunes.

Mother's Day/Father's Day

Song: "He/She's Got the Whole World in His/Her Hands," or "Today."
Read: Homemade prayers written for Mom or Dad beforehand.
Read: Children's book, *Are You My Mother?* by P.D. Eastman, or any other children's book with the theme of loving parent.
Mother or Father: Spontaneous prayer of thanksgiving for family, including why being a parent is such a joy.
Litany to Mary, our mother, or private notes of love to honored parent.
Presentation of Mother's/Father's gifts.
Song: Mom or Dad's choice.

End of School/Beginning of Summer

Song: "Gonna Sing, My Lord."
Homemade litany: Each person is responsible for preparing beforehand 10 thank-you's for the school year and 10 prayers for the summer vacation; family responds with, "Lord, hear our prayer."
Summer resolutions: Share individual and family resolutions beginning with, "This summer I want to . . ."
Drawing: Divide a paper into four parts and each person draws two blessings from the past school year and two of summer.
Song: "Day by Day."

Ascension Thursday

(If weather permits, do this outside. It's fine for the mountains, seashore, camping, or back yard.)

Song: "And I Will Raise Him Up."
Scripture: Acts 1: 6-9.
Close Bible and eyes and meditate for a few minutes.
(See chapter on meditation.)
Lie on backs and share cloud shapes: "Does anyone see Jesus?"
Lazy family sharing: "If Jesus came back today, what shape would he be in?" Example: "I think he'd come back as a school bus driver because ..."
Closing prayer: Apostles' Creed.
Song: "Alleluia."

Pentecost

Song: "Blowing in the Wind" or, "We are One in the Spirit."
Activity: Decorate Pentecost candles—one each with symbols of Pentecost—dove, tongues of fire, light, words, wind, rooftop, etc.
For dinner: light all your candles together and sing, "To Be Alive."
Prayer together:
  "Come, Oh Holy Spirit, fill the hearts of the
  faithful and kindle in them the fire of your love.
  Send forth your spirit and they shall be created,
  and you shall renew the face of the earth.
  Oh, God, who has taught the hearts of the faithful
  by the light of the Holy Spirit,
  grant that in the same Spirit,
  we may be always truly wise
  and ever rejoice in his consolation.
  Through Christ, our Lord. Amen.
Closing Song: "On the Wings of a Dove."

A May Ritual to Mary

Song: "Immaculate Mary" or "Mother Beloved."
Activity: Family together builds a shrine to Mary for the month of May. Each member takes turn putting

fresh flowers or little pebbles around the shrine daily. This ritual is the day the shrine is dedicated.

Prayer: Option of traditional litany or novena to Mary, or a family rosary or spontaneous prayers. (See also prayers to Mary elsewhere in this book.)

Parent: Tells the story of Mary and adds some of the rituals parents remember from their childhood, like the May crowning.

Closing prayer: The Memorare

Closing song: "Song of Mary."

Wedding Anniversary

Song: "Sunrise, Sunset" or the parents' favorite love song.

Activity: sharing of wedding photos.

Parents: Tell about the wedding—how they chose the date, who was there, who celebrated Mass, etc. Children love to hear these details.

Reading from Children's Bible: Marriage Feast at Cana

Parents: Touch hands and recite vows.

Children: Present prayers and/or gifts

Family joins hands and sings: "The Wedding Song" (Peter, Paul & Mary) or any other favorite song appropriate to an anniversary.

Fourth of July

(Do this one at a picnic or outside, if possible.)

Song: "This Land is Your Land."

Children: Present flag; take turns telling what 4th of July signifies.

Family pledge of allegiance.

Spontaneous prayers from each for needs of our nation today.

Closing: A medley of songs such as, "America the

Beautiful," "God Bless America," "Battle Hymn of the Republic," "Star Spangled Banner," and "America."
Shoot fireworks together.

Back to School

Song: "To Be Alive."
(See chapter on School Prayers for following)
All: Say together the Parent-Teacher-Student litany
All: A Prayer Before the First Day of School
Activity: Each child shows new school supplies, tells about teacher, and family responds with a Hail Mary for each child's year.
Drawing: A picture of what each person will be doing the following day—including parents.
Closing song: "Whatsoever You Do."

All Saints

Song: "When the Saints Come Marching In."
Collect: All statues of the saints and put them in the center of the family circle.
Reading: Beatitudes, Matt. 5: 1-12.
Together: New Beatitudes for today's "saints" example: "Blessed are they who pick up litter, for they shall keep our land clean," etc.
If the family does not have nameday rituals, this is a good day to tell the story of each namesake saint.
Drawing: A favorite saint; exhibit and explain
       or
read from a children's saints book
       or
make a family saint poster or banner with each patron saint depicted.
Closing song: "Sons of God."

All Souls

A visit to the church to pray for the souls of deceased relatives and friends is a good family ritual for this day. Before going, make a list of deceased loved ones and go over them with your family. Explain that God wants them with Him in heaven and that we want to ask God to bring them ever closer to Him.

Read Trina Paulus' *Hope for the Flowers,* an endearing book on life, death, and resurrection. Another good story on death and its purpose is Pearl Buck's, *The Beech Tree,* a child's story.
Closing song: "For All the Saints" or "Peace Is Flowing Like the River."

Thanksgiving

(Gather before or after your big dinner but give yourself enough time to do more than say grace before the food gets cold.)
Song: "Here We Are" or "Take Our Bread."
All: Litany of Thanksgiving with each person responsible for ten items.
All: Each offers a prayer for others with whom we can share more of God's gifts and life.
Parent: Asks God's blessing on the family so that it remembers to thank Him for His goodness.
Reading: "Consider the birds of the sky," Matt. 6: 26-30.
Final song: "This Land is Your Land."

Nameday

This is the celebration of the feastday of the child or parent's patron saint. The best book for parents, and well worth the few dollars it costs, is the classic, *My Nameday: Come for Dessert,* by Helen McLoughlin (Liturgical Press, Collegeville, MN). Ask your parish to invest in a few copies if you can't get it yourself. It contains listings of each saint's day, symbols, desserts, recipes and ideas for celebrating.

We celebrate much as we do a birthday, with a cake at the end of the meal and a story about the saint's life.

Through the years we have purchased a book and a statue on each of our children's saints: Teresa, Patrick, and Daniel. (Makes a fine gift at First Communion or First Penance.) We ask the children themselves to draw placemats for the meal with symbols and scenes from their saints' lives. It gives a child familiarity with his or her saint and we ask them to write personal prayers to their patron saints to read right before the cake is cut. This is a good time to invite the godparents, too, if they are around.

E. Jeep

Family Reconciliation or Penance Ritual

Song: "Love One Another" or "Bridge Over Troubled Waters."

Prayer: "Come, Oh Holy Spirit."

Parent: Examination of conscience/meditation:
What have I done to offend God? (a minute's meditation)
What have I done to offend my family?   "   "
What have I done to offend others?   "   "
What have I failed to do as a Christian?   "   "
How can I let Christ's message shine through me?   "   "
What can I do to let God know I am sorry? "   "
What promises do I make to be a better Christian?   "   "

Together: Act of Contrition

Read: The Prodigal Son, Luke 15: 11-32.

Closing prayer: Prayer of St. Francis

Closing song: "Amazing grace."

Parents' Blessing

A lovely family custom is that of the parents' benediction of each child at bedtime. Make a little cross on your child's forehead when tucking the child in or saying goodnight and say this beautiful blessing from scripture: (Numbers 6.)

The Lord bless thee and keep thee,
The Lord make his face shine upon thee,
And be gracious unto thee:
The Lord lift up his countenance upon thee,
And give thee peace.

(Advent, Christmas, and Epiphany are found in another chapter.)

Remember, readers, my emphasis on tailoring a ritual to fit your own family. If you don't know or like the songs I suggest, substitute some family favorites. Add prayers, subtract drawings, modify these celebrations as the Spirit moves you (because He does). If you are beginning ritualizers, don't try to do all of these but choose a few that you feel your family will respond to most readily. Then, as your children ask for more, try a few more. Keep them short, reverent and intimate. You'll wonder why you waited so long to celebrate God together in your home.

5
Lent, Holy Week, and Easter

A Family Lenten Prayer

Jesus, who went out into the desert to fast and pray, invade our hearts and our home during this Lent. Be with us daily, increasing our self-discipline, hearing our prayers and calling our attention to the good that we fail to do. Call us to be better people of God by praying and sacrificing 40 days in you and with you, forever and ever. Amen.

Last year I visited some friends and before I had even removed my coat, one of the small children proudly led me to their family Lenten calendar. Fashioned like a large Advent calendar with little doors taped shut, it was displayed on a prominent wall in the kitchen.

"Every night we get to open a door," little Tony told me.

"And what do you do then?" I asked.

"Oh, we Lent," he replied.

I've thought of his answer many times since. I've never heard Lent used as a verb but it's a perfect use for it because it is an action word. How many families actually "Lent" today? Oh, many of us talk about it and most of us wish we did when it gets near Good Friday or Easter, but I'm afraid many children are growing up without any real experience of Lent.

When we were children, we didn't necessarily like Lent but we observed it. And I think it was good for us. It was a time of spiritual renewal of self, family, and parish. It brought us together in prayer and in ritual. Even families who prayed little the rest of the year took time out for prayer and sacrifice in Lent.

How does a family go about Lenting again? In this chapter, I suggest some of the old and some of the new rituals that can be used in the family during Lent. You'll notice that I spend more time on bringing the spirit of Lent into the home than bringing the family into the church. That is not to minimize church observances but to supplant them at home.

Let's begin with Ash Wednesday. Our home Ash Wednesday ritual has been a longtime favorite in our family. We begin by making some kind of Lenten shrine or centerpiece that stays in a prominent area of the dining room. It varies from year to year. One year, my daughter took a large round tray and divided it into pie-shaped sections. One she filled with cinnamon sugar to symbolize the desert into which Jesus went out to pray. (I regret to say that the sugar steadily disappeared during the six weeks, possibly because we gave up desserts during Lent.) In one section she put a small crown of thorns made of rose branch. In the others she put a cross, a little lamb, a towel bearing an image of Jesus' face, and a little mound of ashes. It was a convenient centerpiece because we could move the tray easily from buffet to table when we had subsequent weekly Lenten rituals.

Other years we have had shoebox tableaux of the type the children make at school. One that my son made sat horizontally on the table and had the Stations of the Cross drawn around the inside (little hands can do that—big adult hands can't) and the empty tomb made of clay on the base of the box. It was not only effective but it was also portable.

Let's talk here a bit about the value and the artistry of these centerpieces. We don't use the word "shrine" much any more but that's essentially what these are. The shrines of our childhood had two disadvantages to the celebrating family of today. They were personal and they weren't made to be portable, so that the family had to go to the shrine. Generally, most of us had one in the corner of our room or the garden and it was considered our shrine.

Sometimes, of course, the whole family created a shrine and had some kind of Lenten or Mary ritual around it and that's the prototype of centerpiece I'm suggesting. We use centerpiece over shrine simply because it best describes it in today's language. We talk about centerpieces for our parties and other celebrations so why not for a religious ritual?

Fashioning the centerpiece is a prayer in itself for the child and/or family. It's great fun for children to sit with parents and create something that is actually going to be used in a celebration. Don't just instruct your child to make a centerpiece but help him or her plan it and create it, if you are invited to do so.

We generally begin to plan for Ash Wednesday a week or so in advance, asking the children and ourselves to clear that evening for our opening-of-Lent ritual. Then we talk about the centerpiece, ask for volunteers to create one, and offer to help. If more than one child wants to try his hand, we either suggest they unite efforts or ask each to create something. If we end up with three, we put one in the living room, one in the dining room, and one in a bedroom and alternate using them.

1. After dinner cleanup on Ash Wednesday, we gather around the Lenten centerpiece at the dining room table and open with, "The Lord of the Dance," one of our favorite Lenten hymns.

2. Then we discuss Lent, what it means, and how it came to be observed.

Lent means spring and it goes back to the early

Church when the new Christians-to-be were preparing to be baptized on Easter. They were called catechumens and during the 40 days prior to Easter, they repented, studied, and sacrificed.

Gradually, when infant baptism became common, Lent became a time of repentance and renewal for all Christians. It is also loaded with symbolism of the Old Testament when the Jews were waiting for their Savior. Passover, which we will observe on Holy Thursday, set the stage for the Mass.

The 40 days, of course, came from Jesus' going out into the desert for 40 days before his time of trial and crucifixion.

Throughout the years, many customs have sprung up during Lent. Spring housecleaning is one. Remember that the Jews had to eat unleavened bread during Passover? Well, this meant they cleaned out their homes of all old bread and prepared themselves for the new spring, their homes as well. Gradually, this became a Christian Lenten practice.

In some countries, children plant grass seed in boxes on Ash Wednesday and put it in a dark place so that it will grow up white and then they take it to church on Easter and the whole altar is white.

The idea of ashes comes from the old form of penance where the person publicly wore sackcloth, a cheap and uncomfortable kind of shirt, and rubbed ashes onto himself to show the world he was repenting for some sin.

3. Next we make a Lenten chain. Whoever is responsible for materials passes out strips of white paper about one by six inches in size, two to each person. We discuss what we would like to do as a family to renew ourselves (see list of suggestions later on in chapter), and when we decide upon five items for the first week, we staple them into a Lenten chain. Then we add five more personal pledges of renewal and add them on to the chain, which we drape around the centerpiece. Each week we add 10 links to our chain so

that by Good Friday, when we staple the ends of the chain together, we have 60 links or so. Instead of the chain, some families make a large cross and tape pledges to it. Others fashion a Lenten calendar like Tony's.

4. We read about the first fifth of Exodus, the story of Moses. During subsequent weeks, we will read about the Pharaoh, slavery of the Jews, and the plagues, all of which lead up to Passover, which we read on Holy Thursday night. Any good children's bible tells the story excitingly and offers good pictures. See the bibliography for more information on bibles.

5. Jim chars a bit of last year's palm from Palm Sunday and places a cross on each of our foreheads with the words, "Remember, you are dust and to dust you will return."

6. We don't end with a song this night and we don't watch television. It is a somber but appropriate tone with which to start Lent.

7. Pass out a pretzel to each person. This is a Lenten symbol, originally made of water, flour, and salt in the form of arms which are crossed in prayer. In Latin, *bracellae,* from which the word pretzel is derived, means arms. We each put our Ash Wednesday pretzel in a prominent place in our own room.

Family suggestions for Lent

Give up sodas, beer, coffee, or tea one day a week.
Walk to work or school or shopping one day a week.
Make a daily visit to church.
Go to Mass once during the week as a family.
Read the bible together 15 minutes daily.
Babysit for a mother who never gets away from home.
Eat one slim meal weekly, really slim, and send the money to the poor.
Go to private confession during Lent or attend a parish penance service.

Say the rosary together weekly.

Give up TV one day weekly.

Shovel the walks or mow the lawn for someone who finds it difficult.

Listen to someone who bores you.

Write a letter to someone who is lonely.

Have a meatless Friday and maybe a sugarless Tuesday.

Make a family Easter banner together.

No desserts? No smoking? No alcohol? No snacks? No salt?

Write a letter to a teacher or pastor thanking him or her for being.

Make a visit a week to the nursing home nearest you.

Volunteer to collect for birth defects or some similar cause in your neighborhood.

Read one spiritual book during Lent privately.

Hold weekly Stations of the Cross at home or attend together in the parish.

Fast one complete day.

Teach your children the prayers they haven't learned.

Have a home Mass.

Set aside one evening weekly just for Lent.

Meditate 15 minutes a day.

Do someone else's chores, such as dishes, one day a week.

At the beginning of this chapter, I told the story of Tony who said, "Oh, we Lent."

Later, Tony's mom explained the Lenten calendar to me. On Ash Wednesday, the family sits together and chooses an action for each day of Lent. Some actions are prayers, some sacrifices, some works to benefit others. "Actually, the calendar is partially yours," she said. "Do you remember your column listing family suggestions for Lent? Well, we just took your list, adapted it to our family, and put it on our calendar. Each evening at bedtime we talk about how we fulfilled our Lenten pledge that day and open the little door for the next day. It keeps us moving on Lent and the children especially love it."

So there is another idea to share with you. I hope your family will begin to Lent, too.

During Lent, try to have some weekly religious ritual at home. The easiest is the Way of the Cross, which I am printing here, but before or after you pray it as a family, check up on how you are doing in renewing and repenting. It's a long time between Ash Wednesday and Holy Thursday and a lot of good intentions can fade if you don't gather and renew weekly.

Family Stations of the Cross

There are several ways you can ritualize the Way of the Cross. Much depends on the age of your children. When our children were very small, we "drew" the Stations on scratch paper while one parent read them. This is fairly effective. Have each person hold up his picture at the end of each Station. In education this is called activity learning and it is an effective way of teaching the Stations. If the same children merely sit and listen to the Stations, they don't get the same impact.

With older children, I suggest you invest in a series of booklets. I list several in the bibliography. If you live near a religious goods store, they have a variety. Or ask your parish coordinator of religious education to order some for you and other families. If none of these work, merely send for some from the publishers listed at the end of the bibliography.

Or simply Xerox the Stations of the Cross following and save them for use annually. Whatever you decide, it's best for each member of the family to have a copy.

A Family Stations of the Cross

All together: Our Jesus, we come together to relive your sacrifice and suffering for us. Send your Holy

Spirit into our hearts and into our midst. *We love you, Jesus, our love. We are truly sorry for having offended you. Never permit us to offend you again. Grant that we may love you always and then do with us as you wish.*

The First Station: Jesus is Condemned to Death

Jesus, you are brought before Pilate to be judged, but he is a weak and cowardly judge. Even though he knows you are innocent, he is afraid of the powerful men who want you dead. So he washes his hands of guilt and condemns you to death.

All: Jesus, never let us be afraid to do the good and right thing even if it means we lose friends or will suffer ourselves in some way. *We love you, Jesus, our love. We are truly sorry for having offended you. Never permit us to offend you again. Grant that we may love you always and then do with us as you wish.*

The Second Station: Jesus Accepts His Cross

The heavy cross is thrust upon you, dear Jesus, and you feel the rough heavy wood against your shoulders. You must carry your own means of death to the hill but you do so freely to save us.

All: Jesus, never let us hesitate to take up our own cross, be it a disappointment, illness, or loss. You have shown us how to accept the cross with love. *We love you, Jesus, our love. We are truly sorry for having offended you. Never permit us to offend you again. Grant that we may love you always and then do with us as you wish.*

The Third Station: Jesus Falls the First Time

How embarrassing it must have been, Jesus, to fall under the weight of the cross. You knew everyone was watching you—you, the man so many were honoring with palms just a few days before. It must have hurt to fall, too.

All: Jesus, let us feel your hurt and humiliation. Let us know that we often hurt and humiliate others deliberately and that isn't what you want us to do. Rather, you ask that we love one another. *We love you, Jesus, our love. We are truly sorry for having offended you. Never permit us to offend you again. Grant that we may love you always and then do with us as you wish.*

The Fourth Station: Jesus Meets His Mother

How awful it must have been for you and Mary, too, Jesus. You knew she was suffering for you, this mother who wiped away little hurts of your childhood with a kiss and a care. Along with your big hurts of the cross, you had to worry about her pain on seeing you suffer.

All: Jesus and Mary, you showed us how to love in the midst of pain and degradation. Let us always stand up to love even if it's the unpopular thing to do. *We love you, Jesus, our love. We are truly sorry for having offended you. Never permit us to offend you again. Grant that we may love you always and then do with us as you wish.*

The Fifth Station: Simon Helps Jesus Carry the Cross

Simon was grabbed out of the crowd to help you carry your cross, Jesus, but he didn't want to do it. How many times do we refuse to help others in pain and need? Simon was lucky. He didn't know he was helping the Son of God.

All: Jesus, let us see yourself in everyone we meet. When we are tempted to pass them by even though we know they are hungry or disadvantaged, nudge us as the soldiers did Simon and give us the privilege of carrying your cross. *We love you, Jesus, our love. We are truly sorry for having offended you. Never permit us to offend you again. Grant that we may love you always and then do with us as you wish.*

The Sixth Station: Veronica Wipes the Face of Jesus

A woman—a mere woman in a time when women were considered nothing—gathered up the courage to run out and wipe your face, Jesus. In exchange for her love, you gave us your image on the towel.

All: Jesus, Imprint yourself on ourselves. Help us to be courageous when we see others suffering, just as Veronica was courageous in wiping your face. She could have been killed. Instead she was blessed. *We love you, Jesus, our love. We are truly sorry for having offended you. Never permit us to offend you again. Grant that we may love you always and then do with us as you wish.*

The Seventh Station: Jesus Falls the Second Time

The cross is getting heavier and heavier. Your strength is ebbing away. Yet, there is a long way to go. You fall and the soldiers prod you up again to continue your journey.

All: Oh, Jesus, it's hard to think about your pain and the weight of the cross. We say that if we were there we would help you. But what if you were walking down our street right now and all our friends were taunting you? Would we help you, or would we join in with the crowd? *We love you, Jesus, our love. We are truly sorry for having offended you. Never permit us to offend you again. Grant that we may love you always and then do with us as you wish.*

The Eighth Station: Jesus Comforts the Women Who Cry for Him

Your friends, the women, who listened to you in the streets and on the hilltops a few weeks ago, cry when they see your suffering. But, always thinking about others, you stop and comfort them.

All: Jesus, comforter of all, help us to do more than

cry for others. When we see cruel treatment of you in others today, give us the courage to stop it. Teach us to comfort those who are unloved in our world. *We love you, Jesus, our love. We are truly sorry for having offended you. Never permit us to offend you again. Grant that we may love you always and then do with us as you wish.*

The Ninth Station: Jesus Falls the Third Time

Your strength is gone, Jesus, and you know it. You wonder if you can make it to the top of the hill. The soldiers poke and prod you with cruel taunts.

All: You must have wished to die there on the ground, dear Jesus. How cruel of the soldiers to taunt you. Help us to remember your perseverence. Help us to get up again when we have fallen from your love. *We love you, Jesus, our love. We are truly sorry for having offended you. Never permit us to offend you again. Grant that we may love you always and then do with us as you wish.*

The Tenth Station: Jesus is Stripped of His Clothing

As if you weren't humiliated enough, you were forced to disrobe in front of everyone, Jesus. Even your clothes were taken away from you. Still, you showed us how to die with dignity.

All: You died with nothing, Jesus ... with no money, no friends to save you, no honor, no clothes even. Were you telling us something? That these things aren't really very important but that the love of God is? *We love you, Jesus, our love. We are truly sorry for having offended you. Never permit us to offend you again. Grant that we may love you always and then do with us as you wish.*

The Eleventh Station: Jesus is Nailed to the Cross

How terrible the pain must have been, Jesus. We

hope that you were numb by then so that you didn't feel every blow. Even so, you were still thinking of us by saying to your Father, "Father, forgive them for they know not what they do."

All: Teach us to forgive as you forgave, Jesus. Sometimes we hoard little resentments and dislikes. Then we realize how you forgave and we take a tiny step toward love instead. *We love you, Jesus, our love. We are truly sorry for having offended you. Never permit us to offend you again. Grant that we may love you always and then do with us as you wish.*

The Twelfth Station: Jesus dies on the Cross

You have died for us, Jesus. For that you came into the world. In the words of the Mass, it is a death you freely accepted. How can we ever thank you?

All: By your death, teach us to face death fearlessly, Oh Jesus. Help us to grieve with others who need us. Help us to stop the senseless deaths of war and greed. *We love you, Jesus, our love. We are truly sorry for having offended you. Never permit us to offend you again. Grant that we may love you always and then do with us as you wish.*

The Thirteenth Station: Jesus is Taken Down From the Cross

Mary, you who held the infant Jesus in Bethlehem, again held your bruised son in your arms in death. How terribly sad you must have been.

All: Hail Mary, mother of God, pray for us sinners now and always. Teach us to love as you loved Jesus and he loved you. *We love you, Jesus, our love. We are truly sorry for having offended you. Never permit us to offend you again. Grant that we may love you always and then do with us as you wish.*

Fourteenth Station: Jesus Is Placed in the Tomb

Your suffering stopped, Jesus, and you lay in the tomb until that glorious first Easter morning. How joyful your disciples. How rejoicing your mother.

All: Jesus, you have died, you have risen, you will come again. *We love you, Jesus, our love. We are truly sorry for having offended you. Never permit us to offend you again. Grant that we may love you always and then do with us as you wish.*

For many people, the old Lent was the only time they went to confession. Lent is an appropriate season for penance and confession. Instead of the Stations of the Cross one week, have a Family Reconciliation Ritual. It will be meaningful and will prepare your family for a parish penance service as well. There is a Family Reconciliation Ritual included in the chapter, "Through the Year with Family Ritual."

Holy Week

Today's parents have strong memories of Holy Weeks past. These were somber weeks, filled with sacrifice, prayer, and reflection. Much time was spent in church—Holy Thursday Mass or service, the traditional Tre Ore (Three Hours) on Good Friday with the Stations, sermons on the Seven Last Words of Christ, kissing of the foot of Jesus on crucifixes held out by the priests, and the incense-led removal of the Host from the altar until Easter Sunday.

Much of that is changed but the spirit of Holy Week can be preserved in the family and parish if some effort is taken.

Some parishes have a meaningful Holy Thursday Mass followed by a parish supper but the experience is so mammoth in many large parishes that confusion rather than community marks the attempt. I much prefer the family Holy Thursday ritual.

Holy Thursday

We combine the Seder or Passover meal with the Last Supper observance to give our family a special sense of being doubly chosen, Old Testament and New Testament people. There are many Seder rituals available today. The one I have following is one that fits our family. Parts are borrowed from other rituals. Perhaps your director of religious education will be giving you a different ritual. Whatever is most comfortable with your family is the one to choose.

If, during Lent, your family has read the story of the Jews trying to escape the tyranny of Pharaoh and slavery, your family will be more understanding of the meaning of Passover, the "passing over" of the Angel of Death who came to strike down the firstborn sons of the Egyptians but not the Jews. After this terrible plague, Pharaoh let the Jews go with Moses to the Land of Promise. If your family hasn't read the whole story of the plagues and Pharaoh, tell the story briefly and read from a good children's bible the story of the Passover night itself.

Preparing for the Holy Thursday Passover meal should be a family affair, not mom's job. Here are some of the duties that can be delegated earlier in the day to various children.

Painting the Passover symbol: God instructed Moses to have his people strike with lamb's blood the top and the two side posts of the doorways of their houses so that the Angel of Death would recognize them as houses of the Jews and pass over them. Our youngest child takes a fat red felt marking pen and paints on three pieces of paper a symbol that resembles a tic/tac/toe with an open top but any symbol could be used, even a lamb or unleavened bread or Angel of death. He hangs one on the outside of the front door, one in the dining room where our Passover meal is to be, and one on the back door.

Unleavened bread: This can be made or purchased.

We usually buy Matzos, which is the flat salted cracker that can be found in the kosher section of the supermarket, but Rye Krisp or any other flat cracker will do.

Charoset: This is a mixture of chopped apples, honey and wine. It symbolizes the mortar the Jews used in building the pyramids for the Egyptians. An older child can easily be responsible for this.

Bitter herbs: Usually horseradish. Symbolizes the bitterness of slavery.

Parsley: symbolizes spring.

Hard-boiled egg and lamb bone: complete the Seder plate. Put one child in charge of both. Don't worry about it if it isn't a lamb bone. Just save a bone from your Sunday chicken or roast in advance. The egg symbolizes new birth and the lamb bone sacrifice. The egg can be sliced into as many slices as there are family members.

Lamb: We always have lamb on Passover night because it is so highly symbolic. Sometimes if the company and the budget merit it, I'll cook a leg of lamb. More often it's lamb chops or lamb stew.

Table: This night calls for your very best *unless* your children are very young. Then put on an older tablecloth. Move the family to the setting you use for important dinners like family Christmas or Thanksgiving dinners. Bring out the good china and silverware. Make a ceremony of preparing for the Passover. Our religious ancestors did. Everyone helps set a lovely table. A centerpiece which captures something of the Passover and the Holy Thursday meal can be crafted by you or that creative junior higher who's lounging in the doorway wanting to be asked to be part of it all. A pretty tray with a wine glass and little loaf of bread and some representation of a lamb would be ideal.

Lamb cake: We are fortunate in having a friend who bakes lamb cakes out of a mold for us and several other friends on Holy Thursday. We use this as our centerpiece. If you don't want to get a mold, just bake a round cake and outline lamb-looking features with icing. Tuck on some pink construction paper ears and you have a lamb—if you cock your head and squint a little.

Guests: Passover/Holy Thursday is a fine time to invite some of your close friends, godparents, and relatives, but you don't want a large crowd. That detracts too much from the intimacy of the observance. Church people who live alone love being part of this dinner. One child can be the official inviter, calling or sending the invitations.

Wine: Because this is one of the few occasions we permit our children to drink a small glass of wine, we get a sweet Mogan David type wine. When they were younger, we used grape juice. There's not much difference in taste. It merely adds to the ritual if real wine is used and they are permitted to taste a little.

Preparing the Seder Plate: Directly before the meal, assemble these on a pretty tray: hard boiled egg, lamb bone, parsley, bitter herb, matzos, and charoset. If there are many at dinner, you can arrange small individual Seder plates but we prefer the sharing of the larger one.

Mother lights candles.

The Celebration

Dad: Tonight we celebrate the Passover when God said to Moses in Egypt:
"Tell my people: every family must find a lamb. If a family is too small to eat a whole lamb, it should share a lamb with another family. The lamb must be young and without a mark on it. It may be either a goat or a sheep."

Child 1:   "Slay the lamb and take some of its blood to put on the doorposts and lintel of every home of my people. That night they shall eat its roasted meat with bitter herbs and unleavened bread."

Child 2: "This is how you should eat it: with your sandals on and your staff in hand, like those in flight. It is the Passover of the Lord. On that same night I will send the angel of death through Egypt, striking down the first-born of the land, both man and beast, punishing the gods of Egypt."

Child 3: "But the lamb's blood on your houses will save you. I will pass over you; thus, when I strike the land of Egypt, nothing will hurt you. This day will be a great feast for you, which your children's children will celebrate.

Seder plate is passed and each item is explained. Family proceeds with meal. When finished, remove all but bread and wine.

Parent: And so it was that before Passover, Jesus knew it was time for him to pass from earth to his Father in heaven. And so, during supper, Jesus, leaving us himself as a new sacrifice, took the bread, broke it, and giving thanks said,

All: "This cup is the new covenant in my blood. Drink this in memory of me."

Parent: This bread and wine are but symbols of the holy sacrifice, and we recall that each year our ancestors celebrated as we are celebrating tonight, first the Passover and later the Last Supper on Maundy Thursday.

Parent: And each Sunday we rejoice that we share in the Body and Blood of Christ at Mass which was begun tonight hundreds of years ago.

Each person takes some bread and wine. Candles are extinguished. All sing "This Is My Body" or some other suitable hymn.

Good Friday

Many families prefer to go to the parish service on

Good Friday afternoon or evening. Others prefer to stay home and observe the afternoon in a family religious tradition. For years, we invited three other families and held a modified Living Way of the Cross. We used the format for the Stations in this chapter but we asked one family to bring large paper crosses to be pinned on the backs of each child and participating adult, one family to furnish a Veronica towel with the image on it, and another to furnish a non-piercing crown of thorns.

Our children, as part of their Holy Week preparation, drew the Station numbers and placed them in different rooms around the house or outside if the weather permitted.

The ritual itself was enriched by asking parents to take the parts of Pilate, Simon, Veronica, and others. At the Fourth Station, each mother received her own little "Jesus." After one disastrous experience, we had the children genuflect instead of fall and we passed over the nailing to the cross which we felt was too traumatic. However, we held our arms out in a cross position while one parent read the Seven Last Words of Jesus and explained them.

At the "I thirst" words, another parent dipped cotton balls in vinegar and touched the tongues of each. After being taken down from the cross, we sat on the floor in a tomblike posture while someone read the following familiar prayer:

Prayer Before a Crucifix:

Look down upon me, good and gentle Jesus,
while before Your face I humbly kneel and
with burning soul pray and beseech You
to fix deep in my heart lively sentiments
of faith, hope, and charity, true contrition
for my sins, and a firm purpose of amendment.
While I contemplate, with great love and
tender pity, Your five most precious wounds,

pondering over them within me and calling to mind the words which David, Your prophet, said of You, my Jesus: "They have pierced My hands and My feet;
they have numbered all My bones." Amen.

Although our children are too grown up for this now, they still talk about our Good Friday Stations with meaning. For those who might be tempted to try it, here are the Seven Last Words on the Cross:
"Father, forgive them, for they know not what they do."
"Mother, behold thy son. Son, behold thy mother."
"This day thou shalt be with me in heaven."
"My God, my God, why have you abandoned me?"
"Father, into your hands I commend my spirit."
"It is consummated."
An optional way of observing Good Friday in the family is to read the Passion account together. If possible, borrow some of the parish missalettes and assign roles to each member of the family. Open with a prayer and read the Passion slowly and with meaning.

A special note here: At the end of each Holy Week, the parish missalettes are usually thrown away. This is a good time to build up your family ritual library. Passover and Passion, as well as Advent and Christmas prayers, can just as well be read from last year's missalettes as this year's. Ask your pastor or director of religious education if you can take some home with you at the end of the week to save for next year's Holy Week.

Easter

Easter is not a private family ritual but one that should be celebrated joyously at Mass with fellow parishioners and later, at dinner, with friends and relatives. If you belong to an ethnic group that has special Easter customs, such as the Polish custom of having the Easter foods blessed on Holy Saturday, by all means pass those customs on in your family.

An old custom familiar to many cultures is that of decorating Easter eggs. We like to do this together on Holy Saturday. Instead of just dyeing the eggs, try decorating some of them with religious symbols—the tomb, cross, rising sun, Easter lily, etc. Choose the favorite of each child and make a centerpiece for your Easter dinner.

Decorate an Easter candle with similar symbols together.

Some families like to make an Easter bread for breakfast that morning. An old Italian custom bakes a whole egg—shell and all—in the top crust. If this idea appeals to you, an easy way to do it is to buy the frozen bread dough, thaw, and braid two loaves into one. Prick an egg and place it in the center of the top crust just before baking. When bread is slightly warm, glaze it with a powdered sugar icing. If you let the kids help braid and glaze it, they will enjoy it more on Easter morning.

6
Advent, Christmas, and Epiphany

I Have Come to Bring You Peace

I have come to bring you peace
Not the peace of the season, for it is too fleeting
Not the peace of the carol, for it is nostalgic
Not the peace of the greeting card, for it is too
    slick
Nor the peace of the crib, for it is too wistful.

Rather, I have come to bring you peace
Peace of the ordinary, the daily, the homely
Peace for the worker, the driver, the student
Peace in the office, the kitchen, the farm.

I have come to bring you peace
The peace of accepting yourself as I have
    fashioned you
The peace of knowing yourself as I know you
The peace of loving yourself as I love you
The peace of being yourself as I am who am.

I have come to bring you peace
The peace that warms you at the completion of a
    task
The peace that invades you at the close of the day
The peace that sustains you at the beginning of
    the day

**The peace that reinforces when you reconcile with
another
The peace that touches you when your family is in
order.**

**Without peace, my coming is unfulfilled.
Without peace, my birth is forgettable.
Without peace, Christmas is a contradiction.**

I have come to bring you peace.

The more I work with parents the more I discover a universal feeling of disappointment in the family observance of Christmas. "Every year we say that we're going to focus on the meaning of the Nativity," said a typical parent, "and by the time we get around to that focus, we're so caught up in the programs and gifts and parties that we never quite get around to Jesus."

Too many other parents respond to her experience for me to dismiss Christmas with a few hymns and prayers. If Christmas is to mean anything in the Christian family, it must be joined with Advent and Epiphany. They are a trilogy, separate but linked. Yet, in my experience, few families observe Advent and even fewer Epiphany.

The main problem with Advent is that it was so poorly observed in the past. Even families who tried to initiate Advent Wreath rituals—and they were few— found the words sterile and uncomfortable in the family. Happily, that has changed and the new Advent rituals are much more meaningful to the family with children of differing ages.

In this chapter, I will offer three formats for Advent: a traditional Advent Wreath ritual, a Jesse Tree ritual, and a modern Advent ritual format. I suggest you read all three and then choose the parts of those which most fit your family and tailor yourself an Advent ritual that becomes as traditional in your family as the tree.

Consider several factors before you launch into an Advent celebration. First, plan far enough in advance so that Christmas doesn't arrive in your home before Advent does. For so many of us, Advent comes before we're ready. More often than not, the first Sunday of Advent is the Sunday after Thanksgiving, a day given to closing a long weekend, to planning for Christmas cards and gifts, and to football. If the family happens to let that first Sunday slip by, it all too often shrugs its collective shoulders and figures it's too late to start an Advent ritual. Try to start pairing Advent with Thanksgiving in your seasonal mind. When you think Thanksgiving, think also Advent—or the beginning of the Christmas season. We already consider Thanksgiving weekend the beginning of the commercial Christmas season. Why not the beginning of the sacred Christmas season?

Second, presume that there will be evenings that your family will be unable to celebrate Advent. December is filled with school and church programs, parties, and other activities, so it's foolish to think that a family is going to be able to gather together for a month of uninterrupted nightly rituals. Rather, plan to hold an Advent observance on as many evenings as possible in your family and be satisfied with that. Remember my earlier reminder: the ritual is meant to serve the family, not the family to serve the ritual.

Third, strive to vary the evening rituals. We take turns planning Advent celebrations in our family so that the routine doesn't become meaningless. I believe this was one of the problems with the old Advent Wreath ceremony. It was so structured that by the 14th evening, it was simply boring. Even the youngest child can offer a refreshing change of pace to the evening ritual, particularly Advent, which is an understandable ritual to children.

Fourth, try to emphasize the idea in your home that Advent is the foundation upon which Christmas is built. Stress the feeling of emptiness of people who have only tinsel and gifts for Christmas because they don't believe in God or have no way of living out that belief. At the same time, don't so over emphasize Advent that the joy and wonder of Christmas gets lost. A practical and effective way of balancing both is by bringing the Nativity into routine Christmas traditions like decorating the tree. More on that later.

Fifth, remember that at this time of the year, which can be hectic and confusing in many families, we long for spaces of quiet and intimacy. Take advantage of this hunger in planning simple Advent and other religious rituals.

Finally, and this is a repeat of an earlier suggestion, keep the rituals short, even shorter than your usual paraliturgies. Children tend to be surfeited with stimulation this month, so don't overdo it. An intimate settling period of 15 minutes with the family around the crib or Advent wreath could be the salvation of sanity in the Christmas family, while simultaneously focusing on the sacredness of the season.

The Advent wreath itself is simply a circle of greens holding four candles. We prefer fresh green boughs but they must be changed to be safe because here in our dry climate of Denver they will dry out too rapidly to keep them for four weeks. Perhaps it is different in moist environment. The base holding the greens can be made of just about anything—wood, styrofoam, or wire from coat hangers bent straight and then formed in a circle. If you have a young boy in your home who is handy, ask him to try his hand at fashioning a wreath base. Ask another child to place the greens on it, and another the candles.

Use three white and one purple or pink candle or, as we do, use four white candles and one with a small purple bow around the base. As a wedding gift we received a Hummel Infant which fits beautifully inside the circle of the wreath. You may have a little crib set or Infant that can be placed reverently inside by little hands, even changed as the season moves on.

On the first day of Advent, point out the symbolism of the wreath.

The four candles represent the 4,000 years prior to

Christ's coming, and, of course, the four weeks of Advent.

The unlighted candles represent the dark ages before Christ's coming. The lighted candles represent Christ, the Light of the World, and their whiteness represents His purity. Each week we light one more candle and that represents the idea that the coming of Christ is closer.

The purple ribbon symbolizes the preparation or penitential aspect of Advent—time for us to get our spiritual selves ready for Christ.

The circular form of the wreath symbolizes that God has no beginning or end, and the green of the boughs indicates hope—the hope of the coming, just as the green of spring indicates new life. The word, Advent, means the coming or the promise.

Traditional Advent Wreath Ceremony

On the first Sunday of Advent, the family gathers for the blessing of the wreath by the father, who begins:

Father: Our help is in the Name of the Lord.

All: Who made heaven and earth.

Father: Let us pray. Oh, God, by whose word all things are sanctified, pour forth Thy blessing upon this wreath, and grant that we who use it may prepare our hearts for the coming of Christ and may receive from Thee abundant graces, through Christ, our Lord.

All: Amen.

He sprinkles the wreath with holy water. The youngest child lights the first candle and the prayer for the first week is said:

Father: Let us pray. Stir up Thy might, we beg Thee, Oh, Lord, and come, so that we may escape through Thy protection and be saved by Thy help from the dangers that threaten us because of our sins. Who livest and reignest for ever and ever.

All:	Amen.
	During the first week one candle is left burning during the evening meal, at family prayers, or at bedtime. Two candles are lighted on the second Sunday, by the oldest child, and allowed to burn as before. The prayer for the second week is:
Father:	Let us pray. Oh, Lord, stir up our hearts that we may prepare for Thy only begotten Son, that through His coming we may be made worthy to serve Thee with pure souls. Through the same Christ, our Lord.
All:	Amen.
	Three candles are lighted on the third Sunday and during that week by the mother. The prayer is:
Father:	Let us pray, We humbly beg Thee, Oh, Lord, to listen to our prayers and by the grace of Thy coming, bring light into our darkened minds. Who livest and reignest for ever and ever.
All:	Amen.
	All four candles are lighted on the fourth Sunday by the father and allowed to burn as before. The prayer said for the fourth week is:
Father:	Let us pray. Stir up Thy might, we pray Thee, Oh, Lord, and come, rescue us through Thy great strength so that salvation, which has been hindered by our sins, may be hastened by the grace of Thy gentle mercy. Who livest and reignest for ever and ever.
All:	Amen.

That is the traditional Advent Wreath ritual but it is our least favorite, simply because it lacks full participation of the family. Looked at closely, all that a middle child would do for the full four weeks of Advent would be to say, "Amen." The ritual points up the reality of the old home rituals, though. Each was patterned after the Mass with the father taking the place of the priest and the family responding as if they were in the pews. No songs, no spontaneous praying, no stories—simply prayers in the traditional language of the Church. Small wonder so few families found it meaningful.

Why did I include it then? Because it *is* traditional and as such can be very effective if used once or twice during Advent as a sign of tradition. Parents can point out that this was the ritual that came down through the centuries in different countries in different tongues but all praying the same prayers to the same God.

The Jesse Tree Ritual

Although the Jesse Tree is rich in Old Testament lore, it's fairly new to our families as a ritual. Yet, it is one of the most popular with today's families, and it is an excellent way of teaching bible history to our children.

Simply put, the Jesse Tree is Jesus' family tree and the term comes from scripture's "root of Jesse," from which Jesus ultimately sprang. So, while awaiting the coming of Jesus during Advent, it makes a lot of sense to talk about the people who waited throughout history for him: Adam, Moses, and all.

The format following is for a parish or group of families and is the best way I know of opening Advent. Try getting a group of friends or families together in your home the afternoon of the First Sunday of Advent and hold this celebration. If you ask each child to "be" an Old Testament person and to make enough of his symbol for each family there, each family can go home with a whole set of Jesse symbols to use during Advent.

If you can't get a group together, then use the First Sunday of Advent in your own family to fashion symbols together. Gather around the table with construction paper, glue, felt pens, string, and other craft aids.

Using the patterns on page 82, trace the symbols and then create some more of your own, if you like. Our set has as many symbols of biblical people and/or times as there are days in Advent and it increases whenever a young hand itches to create something for Christmas.

Jesse Tree Celebration

Explanation

This celebration is suitable for the family alone or for groups of families. It offers a spiritual dimension for the family as an alternative to purely secular Christmas activities. It's not just a party but, rather, a motivation for some family religious customs.

The value of this depends on the family's preparation. It can be used to institute a continuing nightly Jesse Tree ceremony, bringing in the Old Testament legacy unfamiliar to many of our children. If the party is held on the afternoon of the first Sunday in Advent, the family may proceed to use the format along with or instead of the Advent wreath nightly until Christmas, hanging a symbol and telling the story of each prophet.

Preparation

Two weeks prior to the party, each family chooses a Jesse symbol. The Jesse tree, quite simply, is Jesus' family tree. It consists of symbols of Jesus' ancestors. Some possibilities: Adam: tree, serpent, apple
Noah: ark, dove, animals
Abraham: sword, mountain, torch
Isaac: bundle of twigs, ram
Judith: sword
Jacob: ladder, angels
Joseph: bucket, well, multi-colored robe
Moses: basket, burning bush, lamb, staff, cloud

Daniel: lion
Jesse: root or bush
David: slingshot, harp, 6-pointed star
Mary: lily, crown

During the two weeks, each family prepares for its part in the parish Jesse party by:
Making and bringing its symbol to hang on the parish Jesse tree,
having one member ready to explain the symbol,
having another member ready to read a short biblical account of its prophet,
making name tags (symbolic) for the family plus a few for "adopted" family at the party,
bringing cookies or cupcakes decorated with the symbol.
One family also might volunteer to furnish a Jesse tree, either a large limb or a construction paper, wood, or felt tree large enough to hold the symbols.

Celebration

Opening Song: "The King of Glory Comes" or suitable alternative
Leader: *(Hopefully a parent):* Gives an explanation of the Jesse Tree custom, first explaining what an ordinary family tree is. He follows that with the story that for centuries, Jesus' family tree developed while people hoped and waited for him.
Reading: Isaiah 11:1, 6-7: "A shoot springs from the root of Jesse: . . ."
Song: Angels We have Heard on High
Decoration of Tree: Each head of family identifies his family by surname and symbol. He or she introduces each member of the family to the group. The family reads

the scriptural passage corresponding to its symbol and explains the symbol and hangs it in the tree. It involves as many different children as possible so that while one is reading the account, another is holding the symbol high for all to see and still another hangs it on the tree.

Final song: Joy to the World

Celebration ends with decorated cookies and punch. Furnish plain paper and table space for families to make patterns of other symbols for their own Jesse tree celebration. Encourage them to use it along with the Advent wreath on succeeding nights before Christmas.

The decorated Jesse Tree might be placed on the altar or in the vestibule of the Church during Advent.

Adam: apple

The Jesse tree

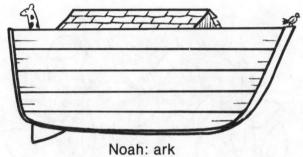

Noah: ark

Moses: cloud

David: harp

Joseph: multi-colored robe

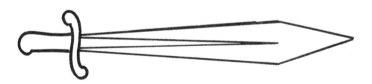

Judith: sword

Art—Ed Curley

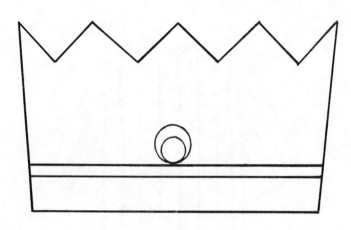

Mary: crown

A Modern Advent Ritual

On the first day of Advent it's a nice custom to bless the wreath as a family. Before lighting the candle, extend all hands over the wreath and say in unison:

> **Blessed are you, Oh, Lord God,**
> **For you give us darkness, hope,**
> **light, and love.**

Opening song: "Prepare Ye the Way of the Lord" (Godspell)
or
"O Come, O Come Emmanuel"
or
any Christmas carol

Reading: Either a little Bible story out of a book like the *Purple Puzzle Tree* or *Arch Books* or the story of Elizabeth (Luke 1:5-24, 39-80), Mary and the Angel

	(Luke 1:26-38) or the birth of Jesus (Luke 2:1-21).
Activity:	Draw a picture of some event leading up to the Nativity or of your family's pre-Christmas preparations. Share.
	or
	Write a promise to a secret Advent friend in the family, to do something especially nice for him or her.
	or
	Write a homemade family Advent litany (see chapter on spontaneous prayer).
Prayer:	Maybe short meditation or a spontaneous prayer of some type.
Jesse:	Have one child reach into the Jesse box and remove a symbol and try to tell what it means. Suspend the symbol from a tree or doorway.
Crib:	Have one child dip into the crib or creche box and take out a figure, gradually building the Nativity scene during Advent. Save the Infant for the last Advent ceremony.
Song:	Any Christmas carol.

The above ritual, as you can see, is extremely flexible. We make it even more so by rotating leaders and we try to outdo each other in creativity. Sometimes we turn out all the lights except the Advent candles and think aloud together how it must have been waiting all those years for the Savior or how it was in the manger that night. Once, our daughter obtained a long sheet of freezer paper and we spent the whole evening drawing a Christmas mural together. It was a lot of fun and nobody wanted to quit.

We laugh when we recall one Advent when our youngest was very young indeed but wanted his turn to lead the ritual. The big night came. Under his direction we sang "Gloria"—just the one word—endlessly. Then he told a story of how the Three Kings came to visit Jesus in a dune buggy and he was entirely serious. (In the toddler mind, what better way to get over the sand?) Then he had us take the animals out of the crib for a walk around the darkened house. We walked through the rooms dozens of times holding a cow or a sheep and singing "Gloria."

The last evening can be very special. Gather the family and any relatives and friends visiting around the wreath on Christmas Eve, say some prayers, sing some carols and take the Infant from the box and put him in the crib. Allow the Advent candles to burn down.

Christmas

Here are some simple prayers and suggestions designed to turn your secular observances of Christmas into prayerful ones.

A Decorating-the-Tree Celebration. All gather around the bare tree and pray:

> **"Our Father, who gives us trees and all beautiful things, thank you for this tree. Help us to decorate it in excitement and joy in anticipation of your Son's coming. Lead us not onto each other's toes but give us the blessing of realizing how lucky we are to have one another, a tree, and you. Amen."**

When the tree is decorated, turn on the lights and sit on the floor around it as you all extend your hands and bless the tree in these words:

> **"Bless this tree, Oh, Lord God and let it fill us with the wonder and joy of Christmas which is the gift of your Son Jesus to us. Amen."**

Sing a few carols and then put away all the boxes and other litter.

A Wrapping-the-Packages Celebration. Gather around the table laden with tape, colorful bows, and presents. Someone read this prayer:

> **"Fill our hearts with love for the persons who will receive our gifts, Oh, Holy Spirit. Guide our fingers into tying sturdy bows and our souls into an eager anticipation of your rebirth in us, Oh, Jesus. Amen."**

Sing carols as you wrap.

A Baking-Cookies Celebration. Gather in the kitchen, warm with oven smells, around the table dusty with flour.

Make a novena as you roll, cut, decorate and sample—

For safe Christmas traveling, we pray to the Lord:
Lord, hear our prayer.
For many more Christmases together, we pray to the Lord:
Lord, hear our prayer . . . and so on.

Christmas Day

The sacred part of Christmas is very hard to preserve on Christmas Day in the family. The kids are either too excited or exhausted for any more ritual. I really like the growing practice of having a children's Christmas Eve Mass on the afternoon of the day before Christmas and then allowing the children to get into the gift, relative and Santa Claus observance without trying to get them back for a children's Mass on Christmas Day.

If your parish doesn't have a Mass for children, perhaps you could suggest one. Some delightful customs are arising at such Masses. Many have an enactment of the Nativity as the homily by children of the parish. Others have the children bring up gifts which they have made to share with less fortunate children. Others have children invite their grandparents to sit with them and, lacking any grandparents, to substitute someone in the parish or neighborhood.

Epiphany

To complete Advent and Christmas, we need to observe Epiphany and we've had little instruction on how to do this in our Church and culture. For many families, Christmas ends with Christmas Eve Mass. Yet, this is when the real celebration of Christmas should begin.

Take down the tree on the 26th if you like but move the crib to the center of attention. The simple act of moving the Wise Men each evening a bit closer to the crib is a start for Epiphany-minded families. Each evening have a prayer, a bible reading, or a meditation around the crib. Sing some of the carols.

Make a visit with your family to various churches to view their nativity scenes. With your children on vacation, maybe daily Mass is worth considering. Have a spiritual gift-giving on the date—homemade prayers, statues, banners, spiritual bouquets for one another.

Finally, have an Epiphany party in your home during which you exchange your spiritual gifts and take down the crib. Here is a simple ritual:

Song: "You are the Light of the World" or "This Little Light of Mine"

Scripture: The Three Kings story, Matt 2:1-12.
Individual prayer, beginning with, "If I were visiting Jesus today, I would bring him this gift..." Opening and sharing little homemade Epiphany gifts.

Drawing: Each one draws a big star and grants a good wish for the family on the point of each.

Closing song: "We Three Kings."

90

7
Scripture and Meditation in Today's Family

In Prayer it is better to have a heart without words, than words without a heart.

John Bunyon

Two of the fastest growing interests in our Church today are bible study and meditation, and these are the two with which most Catholics are unfamiliar. When today's parents were young, the bible was a Protestant thing. We heard it from the gospels on Sunday and that was enough for us. Meditation was mainly for monks, cloistered nuns, and retreats.

Now we're discovering new excitement in both areas. Catholics are flocking to bible study groups in other churches because they are so much more knowledgeable than we are. They are familiar with scripture discussion techniques and they show a familiarity with the bible that engenders a kind of open love for it that is attractive to all, but young people especially. That is why we are seeing so many of our Catholic youth attracted to campus bible groups. They are finding something there that they haven't found in our churches or homes, and it's more than just a book.

It's a lifestyle based on familiarity with The Book, something new in Catholicism.

At the same time, many youth and adults, too, are finding God in meditation. The immense popularity of transcendental meditation attests to a need for reflection and quieting of ourselves. Certainly our hectic pace of life is one culprit but there's also a hunger for a deeper meaning of life—a search for God in daily life—evident in our culture.

In this chapter I would like to pair the two—scripture and meditation—and give some suggestions for initiating them in your family.

Scripture

If you have young children, invest in some good children's bibles and bible stories. You won't regret it. You'll find yourself reaching for them during rituals and times of quieting. Eventually, your family will begin reaching for them, too.

Years ago I was sent a set of little Bible booklets called *Little People's Paperbacks*. Each contained a simple story and was attractively illustrated for children. The Adam and Eve story, for example, was titled "They Disobeyed" and had a colorful but devious snake on the cover. I am sure these are out of print now but they have been used and reused so much that when I wanted to give them away a couple of years ago, there was a collective protest from my children.

Instead of keeping the little paperbacks with our other bibles and celebration books, I kept them in the children's bookcases. They would reach for them occasionally just as they reached for other books. Many a morning I found one in bed with a child who wasn't supposed to be reading but sleeping the night before.

Two equally attractive sets for young children today are *The Purple Puzzle Tree* books and the *Arch Books* both published by Concordia Publishing House, 3558

S. Jefferson, St. Louis, Mo. 63118. Each has about 25 different books and they are modestly priced, usually under a dollar a book. Most bible bookstores carry both sets. They are delightfully illustrated and on target with language for children under ten.

Standard Publishing Company, 8121 Hamilton Ave., Cincinnati, Ohio 45231, has consistently good bible materials for children as does David C. Cook Co., 850 N. Grove Ave., Elgin, Ill. 60120. A postcard to any of the above three publishers requesting a catalog ought to give you a wide variety of bible books from which to choose. In addition to the stories, they have items like crossword puzzle books on the bible at various age levels.

There are so many good children's bibles that I hesitate to recommend any. The ones most often chosen and read in our family are these:

Children's Bible, Liturgical Press, Collegeville, Mn. This is the familiar little purple bible that we reached for often in the years when our children were small. It is in paperback form and inexpensive, a fine gift, incidentally, for a First Communicant. All of our children read out of it at their First Communion Masses.

The Children's Bible, Golden Press, New York. This is probably the most familiar children's bible because it is easily available in bookstores and libraries. The stories are well written and the illustrations traditional. We use this one more now that the children are older (as of this writing 10, 13, and 17).

Bible Stories, retold by David Kossoff, Follett Publishing Co., New York. This is close to the old bible history stories and good for reading aloud. Some humor and a good deal of suspense can be found in these stories.

Good News for Modern Man is the most popular grown-up New Testament in our family. Part of it, I believe, is that it's a paperback and children are very comfortable with paperback books. The translation by The American Bible Society makes a big difference, too.

Whenever I mention a few specific books, I risk omitting other very good children's and family bibles. I really believe that certain bibles are tailored to certain families and that your best move is to visit several church goods stores and secular bookstores and look over their selection before you invest. If you're buying a hardback Old and New Testament for children, check the binding and make sure it's sturdy. It gets a lot of bouncing around and opening flat on its face.

Once you get the bible or bible stories, what do you do with them? They are immensely valuable during the little home rituals I suggested in earlier chapters. Familiarity is an important part of celebration. Just look at the difference in parish singing when "Holy God, We Praise Thy Name," is sung. It isn't that that particular song is more musical or that the words are more stirring that cause people to sing it. It is because it is familiar to them. It is one of the few hymns that the general congregation sang in the old church, so people know it. Our children will probably react similarly to "Take Our Bread" or one of the church songs of this generation.

Help your family to become familiar with the bible, first through the little bible stories, later through readings, discussions, and meditation. Every time you are going to have a family ritual or even an occasional bedtime prayer time, get out one of the little bible stories.

During Lent, Advent, and other periods of the year, read a little of the bible after each evening meal. Children love the Old Testament stories if they are on their level. In earlier chapters, I suggested using bible stories as an integral part of Advent as in the Jesse Tree ritual, as preparation for the Passover/Holy Thursday meal and for numerous other church holidays.

One of the greatest helps for families is to have parents familiar with the bible. If you count yourself among the thousands of Catholic parents who feel baffled in this area, why not seek out a good bible study group? Ask for one from your parish or get together a group of parents like yourself and find someone to lead you. Lacking that, look into bible groups in the other churches in your geographical area. You will find much ecumenical sharing in scripture classes.

You may have gathered by now that I feel every family should have a religious bookcase or shelf. In this I would include all the bibles, big and little, this book and any others like it, ritual paraphernalia, saints books, old but useful missalettes, religious song sheets (these can be used over and over again), old and present religious textbooks, old missals, your old Baltimore Catechism for reference purposes, religious records, and any religious story books you may have. When one of you is leading a prayer session or ritual, you can go directly to this shelf and have the materials in front of you.

Meditation

Meditation has become a fad in our culture which I suspect will diminish in the years ahead but it's a mistake to think that it is new to our Church. The rosary is a prayer of meditation. The constant repetition of the same prayer while dwelling on a mystery serves much the same purpose as does the mantra in transcendental meditation with the added gift, of course, of bringing oneself into God's presence.

While ours is not a meditating family, I've found that we like very much to settle our minds and bodies with quiet times together around a specific season or reason. For example, one of our favorite Advent rituals is to sit in front of the Nativity Crib with only the lights of the tree glowing in the room and to have a soft carol, a short reading of the Annunciation, and then a period of silence.

It doesn't have to be long. In fact, meditating with children is counterproductive if it is too long. Don't let your silence go much over four or five minutes until your family builds up to it. We've found that merely diminishing the stimulation in the form of lights, noise, and rushing leads to a natural kind of meditation.

The car is a fine place for meditation. We read stories such as *The Velveteen Rabbit* when the children were little and a selection from Anne Frank's *Diary Of a Young Girl* when they were older, and then just thought about it for a few miles before we talked about it. Just as the car is ideal for reciting the rosary, so is it effective for reading scripture. Read the story of the Prodigal Son, for example, and let several miles go by while each person reflects in his or her own mind on how he or she would react as son or father in the same situation. Then open it up for discussion. Many a pleasant mile can be passed in this way.

As I work with parents across the country, I find more meditating families, usually as a result of the parents getting involved in contemplative prayer, yoga, or some other form of meditation. Some families seem better able to pull it off than others. Those who have worked hard to get their families to meditate together tell me to caution families not to expect too much too soon nor to push meditation too strongly.

One father told me, "Actually, we didn't push the kids into it at all. My wife and I took a course in meditating from our diocesan adult education office. Every night after dinner we went into the bedroom and meditated together for 20 minutes. One night our teenager asked if he could join us. From that time on, it was just a matter of which child next. Now we all get involved but not every night."

There are many forms of meditation. For more complete information, I like the section on meditating found in the book by the Green Bay Diocesan Liturgy Commission, *Prayer: Family Style.* If you can get your parish to order a few of these, it's well worth the reading time, or buy your own copy.

For those who can't obtain it, here are some of their suggestions. They list the following Scripture readings "to start you enjoying Scripture":

Luke 10:25-37
Luke 11:5-13
James 2:14-26
James 2:1-13
Matthew 5:21-26
Matthew 5:38-48
Matthew 25:31-46
Mark 10:35-45
John 14:15-31
John 13:31-35
John 15:1-17
I Corinthians 13:1-13

To these I would add some of the more familiar psalms: "The Lord is my Shepherd," (Psalm 23) and Ecclesiastes 3: "For every thing there is a season." Also use any prayer that your family likes. I like to meditate with the Prayer of St. Francis (Chapter I.): "Lord, make me an instrument of your peace..."

Here are some more suggestions for meditating.

1. Write individual prayers about the length of the Hail Mary. Read each aloud and reflect or meditate on it for two or three minutes before going on to another. (Parents, save these prayers and present them to your children when they are parents themselves.)

2. Listen to a popular religious song together: "I Don't Know How to Love Him," or sing a hymn from church and meditate on the words.

3. Read *Hope for the Flowers* by Trina Paulus, and meditate on the caterpillars for a few minutes.

4. Read a parable and have everyone draw a picture of it. Place the pictures on the floor or table so the group can see them and meditate on them.

5. Say "The Apostles' Creed" in segments, stopping after each phrase to meditate on its meaning.

6. Instead of bedtime prayers, sit together quietly and review your day together or examine your consciences with the uses of the questions from the Reconciliation Ritual (Chapter 4).

7. Recite a favorite proverb or poster message:

"Prayer does not change God, but it changes him who prays." Kierkegaard

or

"To the millions who have to go without two meals a day, the only acceptable form in which God dare appear is food." Mahatma Gandhi

8. Take just one thought from scripture and reflect on it: "I am the resurrection and life. Whoever believes in me will live, even though he dies; and whoever lives and believes in me will never die. Do you believe this?" John 11:25-26.

9. Read one of the stories of a saint's life from your saints book. Meditate on how easy or difficult it would be to live that life today.

10. Hold hands, hum *Amazing Grace* for a minute or two. Drop hands. Continue humming, breathing deeply and thinking of a certain scene from Jesus' life such as his baptism by John.

11. Sit around a campfire and tell about the moments in your life when God spoke to you forcefully. After each, stop and meditate while studying the fire.

12. Go out into your backyard on a summer's night and lie down on the cool green grass. Search the stars with your eyes and talk quietly about the vastness of the universe and the wonder of the Creator who fashioned it. Drift off to solitude together.

These are just a few suggestions. None of them may fit your own family's style but keep searching for one or two that appeal to them. Keep in mind one of the expressed hopes of people for a more satisfying life today is for less: less confusion, less noise, less materialism, and less stimulation. We also want more: more time together, more time outside, more quiet time, and more time to get to know ourselves. Why not begin the process in the family?

8
Prayers for Ordinary Days

Prayer for an Ordinary Family

Thank you, God, for an ordinary family with ordinary problems and joys. We don't seek the model marriage, the brightest children, or the best neighborhood. We are content with the gifts you have sent us—normal children, a good marriage, and satisfying work. For these, we thank you. Let your light shine through our ordinariness.

Listening to God

Lord, teach me to learn to listen for you in the many ways in which you speak—
in the phone call from the tiresome neighbor
in the drudgery of housework that will need to be
    redone tomorrow
in the inane and materialistic television commercials
in the flux and fevers of February
in elections, disasters, and deaths
in laughs, nonsense, and joys—
Let me believe, really believe, that you speak to me daily in dozens of voices and forms. Then I won't have to wait for that profound spiritual bolt of light-

ning to know you, but rather we can become good, everyday friends.

For Grandparents

For grandmothers and grandfathers, praise the
   Lord.
For the limitless love they share, for the concern
   they show,
for the prayers they say, for the hope they pass on,
praise the Lord.
For the lines and wrinkles, for the limps and liver
   spots,
for tri-focals and bad knees, for grey hair and bald
   spots
praise the Lord.
For the birthdays they never forget, for the
   afghans they knit,
for the memories they share, for the examples
   they offer,
praise the Lord.
For the babies they hold, for the stories they read,
for the bragging they do, for the pictures they
   show,
praise the Lord.
For the day, pray God, when we will be
   grandparents just like them,
praise the Lord.

To Overcome Inertia

Help me to get moving, Lord. I have boring work to do. I did it last week. I'll have to
do it again next week. Help me to find some
pleasure in it, even if it's only to know that
I've accomplished it. Help me to understand
that there are uninteresting jobs in everyone's life. Teach me not to count how many
times I've done this or how many times I
must continue to do this but rather to thank

you for all the work I do that is not boring.
Help me to get moving, Lord.

Help Him to Make the Team, Dear God

Help him to make the team, Dear God.
Oh, please, help him to make the team.
I know there are lots greater problems in the
   world—
like wars and hunger—
but he doesn't.
Right now, the only world for him is the team.
He's tried twice before and not made it.
He's getting bigger and beginning to doubt himself.
Oh why, dear God, must muscles and coordination
   determine
the self worth of a ten-year-old?
If he doesn't make the team, please,
at least, let him feel worthwhile.
Help him to understand he has many gifts and
   talents that
the tough boys don't have.
And, if there's room for one more favor, God,
would you give him some little way of saving face
   if he doesn't make it?
Maybe a conflicting activity or even a sore mus-
   cle?
You know, a way out, so he can tell his friends and
   himself that
he could have made the team if . . .
Thanks, God, for your patience with a mother who
loves her children a little too much at times.

Prayer to Mother Seton

Congratulations on being a first:
a first American saint who was first a wife

and mother, then a Sister, who went through all the pains of trying to be good in all your roles. Most important to me, you are also the first saint-mother who had children who didn't turn out perfectly.
For that I thank you.
We imperfect parents—or parents of imperfect children—need models of hope. I know you worried about your sons. So do we all. I know that you prayed one back into the fold but that you felt you failed with another. it's comforting to know that even a saint shared our feelings of failure and guilt. Pray, help us to do our best, as you did, and then, to understand God's reasons for permitting us to fail occasionally.

For Something Lost

I can't find it, God. Please help me to think, to recall where I might have put it. I place my trust in you to help me find it. Lead me in that direction. St. Anthony, who has helped us find so many things, I ask for your prayers, too. And when I do find it, let me not forget to thank you.

Rain, Children, and God

It has been raining for eight days, God be praised.
It has ended a period of drought, God be praised.
It has brought new life to the trees, to the ground and the grasses thereupon, God be praised.
Aye, it has been raining for eight days, God be praised.
It will soon cease, God be praised.
It is shortening the life of this greying mother and her penned-up offspring and her coiled nerves.
It will soon cease—God be praised!

A Child's Prayer to Mary

When I am scared or mad or blue,
Help me, Mary, to pray to you.
Because a mother always cares,
I know that you will hear my prayers.

A Mother's Prayer to Mary

It's morning, O Mother of mothers,
and I face an impossible day.
House to clean, groceries to buy,
children to drive, meetings to attend
...miracles to contemplate.
I don't see how I can get through this day
without your help.
Mary, keep everyone well today.
Keep interruptions at a minimum.
Give me the courage to say no.
Most of all, Blessed Mother, nudge me
to recognize the joys of this day,
the glory of God,
and the availability of you.

An Adult's Prayer to Mary

Mary, you said yes and we received.
We say maybe and wander in doubt.
Give us the strength of your faith,
the confidence of your yes
and the courage to live the Good News
as your Son lived and preached it.

For Quieting the Mind and Body

I needed to stop and reflect, so I worked faster.
I needed to think, so I took a class.
I needed to pray, so I read a book.

I needed to retreat, so I called some friends.

Oh God, Creator of silence and solitude, refuse me these escapes from myself and you. Let me heed your call to retreat, to quiet my mind and body, to find peace in your gifts of nature. Help me to be an example of peace and harmony to my family.

Meditation Over a Sick Child

Two a.m. my vespers
cold kitchen my cathedral
rocking chair my kneeler
sick toddler my prayer.

Who needs a retreat master
to explain
those hot little fingers seeking relief
roving constantly from my neck
to my shoulders
to my back and back
are my soul seeking relief
roving constantly around God?

Who needs a canon
and printed formulae
to teach me prayer
when I hear such
loving
trusting
entreating
prayer from parched lips,
"Mommy, mommy, mommy . . . "

Who needs a pulpit preaching patience
when that
and love
is all I can offer?

Who needs lofty lessons on hope
reflected off stained glass windows
on high holy days
when hope
is the divine balm of motherhood?

Press closer, little one, for comfort
as I press closer to God
for your comfort.
Merge into me
losing your pain in me.

Like God
I welcome it.

Whimper why
why
why
the pain?

Dear God
why the pain
all around us?

Why his tiny pain?

Why my mother's anguish
over my helplessness?
Is it to show us
we are helpless?

Ah, Mass is ended
he goes to sleep
wet brow
limp limbs.

From kitchen cathedral
I carry him
to warm crib.

I go in peace
to my bed.

Thanks be to God
for pain
and relief of pain,
which is love.
Amen.

All the Other Kids Are Going

Here we go again, Lord
Long face
Swollen lip
Wounded eyes
Nobody understands her
this first child in all your world
to hear "no."
Ah, the indignity of it all
"My mother won't let me . . . "
"My dad's a square . . . "
"It's too far . . . "
"Too late . . . "
"Too young . . . "
Sob.
Sob away, my child
and if it helps, hate me.
I know your anguish.
Yesterday I, too, railed
at the unfairness of it all.
Too young,
then too poor,
then too married,
then too old
to go.
Go ahead and pout away, my love
for much of life is "no."
And one must rehearse,
I know.

While Working in the Garden

"And he went out to the garden to pray" —
I've always understood that, Jesus. In my
garden cathedral, I see your Father's
remarkable works — the balance of nature,
the sprouting of seeds, the weeds striving
for rightful space, the world in microcosm.
On my knees I work and reflect. My garden
is a prayer, not a perfect prayer, but then,
not a perfect garden, either. I love to work
alone there in the quiet of a cooling late
afternoon. It brings me closer to You,
Jesus, and to your Father who created gardens for our bodies and souls. Let me
always have a garden.

A Mother Thanks You, God

Thank You, God, for September
for it ends endless August
with its
"there's-nothing-to-do's"
and
"I'm telling's"
and
"How-come-I-always-have-to's."

Thank you, God, for 98.6
for it ends endless fevers
and their
complications
and
sunken eyes
and limpid little bodies.

Thank you, God, for Mondays
for they end the weekend
with its

basketball games
and
"everybody's going"
and
"I've got to be there by 8's."

Thank you, God, for bedtime
for it ends the day
with its
morning freshness
and
afternoon homecoming
and
evening sharing.
Thank you, God.

On Family Fighting

Oh, Mother Mary, help me not to yell so much. I couldn't help it. Maybe. After picking up all day, I couldn't stand the sight of those socks and shoes dropped in a parade across the living room. I know I over-reacted and I said some things I shouldn't have said. Give me the courage to apologize, but first let me feel forgiveness.

I'm tired tonight and I'm feeling sorry for myself. Why do I take one's faults out on all of them? They're tip-toeing around out there feeling guilty. Don't let me enjoy that so much. Sometimes I wish I could walk out the door and be responsible for myself alone. No more littered floors. No more bickering children. No more dirty pans.

No more cuddly children? No more shared laughs? No more of those who make my life worth while? I don't really mean it, Mary. But help me not to yell so much, please.

A Parent's Plea

For boys
who care about sports and food
We thank thee, Oh Lord.
For girls
who care about grades and books,
We thank thee, Oh Lord.
From boys
whose favorite subject is recess,
Deliver us, Oh Lord.
From girls
whose favorite subject is boys,
Deliver us, Oh Lord.

What a Beautiful Day It Is

What a beautiful day it is, Jesus. Let me appreciate you in every nerve, every waft of refreshing breeze, every shout of playful noise from my children, every smile from my spouse. Thank you for this day and glory of You in it.

School Prayers

A Prayer Before the First Day of School

Parent: School starts tomorrow, Mary. We put this year in your hands.

Second Parent: We pray that our family will emerge in June more learned, more prayerful, and more compassionate to others.

Child: For my new teacher, _____, that she will like me and I will like her and that I will learn all that I am supposed to in ____ grade.

All:	Please pray to Jesus for us, Mary. (Each child repeats prayer.)
Parent:	That all children everywhere will experience loving teachers and good classes.
All:	Please pray to Jesus for us, Mary.
Teen:	That my school year will be filled with good classes, good friends, exciting school activities and God's love.
All:	Please pray to Jesus for us, Mary.
Parent:	That we have a minimum of illness, missed homework, and missed busses.
All:	Please pray to Jesus for us, Mary.
Parent:	That our children will help new children to be less lonely and less frightened these first days of school.
All:	Please pray to Jesus for us, Mary.
All:	Hail Mary, full of grace, hear our prayer for a school year that will please your Son, educate us, and help us to fulfill God's plan for us in His world. Amen.

Prayer Before Reading to a Small Child

Thank you for this bonus, Lord, this moment of intimacy and sharing between me and my child. Let me savor the quiet joy we give to one another. Help me to make time to read together again tomorrow because the day after tomorrow he will be reading to himself and will be much too grown up to pull my arm around him and open a story that transports us together to another time and place. And for those families who have never read together, I pray, Lord, that they try it just once. Amen.

Parent-Teacher-Student Litany

All: Dear God of all Creation, thank you for the marvelous gift of learning. We beg you to hear our prayers for our school life. Come into our midst, into our minds, and into our hearts.
For school boards and superintendents,
For principals and secretaries, *Response:* **Hear our prayer, Oh, Lord.**
For custodians and bus drivers,
For librarians and cooks,
For teachers and learners,
For buildings and playgrounds,
For budgets and books,
For parents and families,
For assignments and grades,
For programs and games,
For field days and field trips,
For book reports and homework,
For kindergartners and school aides,
For first graders and reading teachers,
For second graders and music teachers,
For third graders and school nurses,
For fourth graders and room mothers,
For fifth graders and speech therapists,
For sixth graders and playground supervisors,
For seventh graders and assistant principals,
For eighth graders and resource people,
For freshmen and activity directors,
For sophomores and coaches,
For juniors and drama directors,
For seniors and counsellors,
Keep us all under your loving eye this year, Lord, and teach us to love one another as we learn from each other.
Mary, mother of all students, pray for us
That we may learn to be what God wants us to be
That we may accept the responsibilities of learning, *Response:* **Pray for us**

That we may support our schools and teachers,
That we may perceive, judge, and act wisely,
That we may grow in age and grace,
That we may furnish educational hope for all,
That we may change the world,
That we may make new friends and keep old friends,
That we may be patient with our students and with
our teachers,
That we may keep our school clean and pleasant,
    Come, Oh, Holy Spirit, and fill the hearts and
minds of your faithful. Grant us faith, knowledge and
perseverance so that we may go forth and spread
the Good News. Amen.

Prayer For a Dropout

Dear God, I am so weary today. My son
dropped out of school. I am a failure. What
did I do wrong? I went to PTA. I checked his
homework—all the right things. What did I
do wrong? Sometimes I think it would be
easier not to be a parent, God. All those
grades, all those truancies, and now this.
For what? What can he do in life? Work in a
gas station? Drive a truck? Yes, I know
somebody has to drive a truck but why
him? He has so much potential. What is
your plan for him? Help me to understand,
please. I feel so alone and such a failure.
Help him to find his way and help me to
accept it. Thank you, God.

A Time For Math

For everything there is a Season,
You taught us, Jesus, our brother.
This season it's modern math
meeting unmodern parents.

Enlighten us, we pray
on Base Ten and Base Four and Thousands
Place and Usual Numerals.

Let us not show our ignorance again
as when we thought Correct Sign
meant Stop on Red.
Help us to understand the bases
and help our daughter to understand
our precocious senility.

A Parent's Prayer for the Teacher

Oh, Mary, mother of the Greatest of Teachers,
fill my child's teacher with patience and
    understanding.
Help her to understand that he tries, even if he
    doesn't always achieve.
I know that she has a class full of students
but
if you could let her know that his stoniness covers
    his humiliation
at times,
or that his awkwardness comes from trying too hard
    to please
or that his exaggerations stem from a need to be
    recognized,
he and I will be forever grateful.
Let me be more patient and understanding of my
    child's teacher, too, Mary.
Teach me to look at both sides of an issue before I
    take my son's word.
Help me to reassure her that she is loved and
    appreciated.
And let me offer to help her when she needs a paper
    correcter,
a cupcake maker, or just a friend who happens to be
    a parent. Amen.

School Program Time

Dear God, let him remember his lines.
Help her reach the high notes.
Don't let him trip.
Or stand mute,
Or cry
Please.

A Girl's Prayer to Teresa of Avila

St. Teresa, who never pretended to be less bright than you were, help me today. Invite me to consider you as model, Oh, Doctor of the Church. Help me rid myself of that obsolete notion that smart girls must play dumb. Let me be proud of my scholarship, not embarrassed. Help me know that the boys and men who count are more interested in my mind than in my hair. Amen.

A Parent's Prayer at Report Card Time

Oh, God, who sent us children of such different
    talents,
help us to appreciate each for what he is.
Help us not to overpraise the scholar and
    underpraise the dreamer.
Inspire us, as parents, to say the right words to let
    them
all know they are loved equally, in spite of their
    grades.
And thank you, God, for not having report cards on
    parents. Amen.

School Dance (Version 1)

Jesus, I want to go to the dance.
But I'm afraid to ask a girl.
What if she says no? What will I say?
What will the guys say?
Why would she want to go with me?
Help me not be so scared, Jesus. She's just a girl.
Just a girl! Like I ask one everyday.
Let her say yes, Jesus. Please let her say yes.

School Dance (Version 2)

Jesus, I want to go to the dance.
But what boy will ask me?
Why would he want to go with me?
My hair is brown. I'm not exactly skinny.
And I'm not a cheerleader.
Still, Jesus, I want to go to the dance so badly.
Let someone ask me, please, Jesus. Please.

School Dance (Version 3)

They're off to the dance, Jesus.
Thank you for their dates. They're so
excited, so awkward, so adolescent, on the
threshold of maturity. Help us to let them
go, Jesus. Part of me thrills at their growing
up, part rebels. They are such children. How
can they go to a long dress dance when
they can't even find their sneakers?
Anyway, let them have a good time tonight.
Keep them out of high speed cars on icy
highways. And out of dark cars on dead-
end roads. Help them to handle any situation that might arise. Keep them in the palm
of your hand, Dear Jesus, and help their
parents realize that they are growing up to
become their own persons.

9
Prayers For Special Days

"There is nothing that makes us love a man
so much as praying for him."
William Law

Home Blessing

Bless our home, and make it fit for Thee, Oh God.
Send your Holy Spirit into each nook and cranny.
Let the walls resound with love and laughter.
Let your birds sing on your trees outside
and your lilies flourish in your gardens.
Bless our kitchen and fill it with the warmth of
    shared bread.
Bless our family room and fill it with loving
    communication.
Bless our bedrooms and fill them with restful
    slumber.
Bless each room and each of us, dear God,
and make yourself at home with us.

Birthday Prayer

For (Tim) who is (8) today, thank you,
Lord, Just as a finger is part of a hand, he is
part of all of us, of our family. Help him to

have a good birthday with lots of love and happiness. Let him have a good year and let us all be together again in good health on this day next year to help him celebrate being (9).

A First Communion Prayer

Bless our First Communicant, Jesus, and invite him/her to be a regular guest at your table. By the sharing of your bread, help him/her to share your life in others. Oh, Lord of the loaves and fishes, who nourishes us all with your bread and your spirit, let us rejoice in this First Communicant and may his/her new life in you bring us ever closer together.

A First Penance Prayer

For your forgiveness, we thank thee, Lord.
For your loving reconciliation, we bless thee, Lord.
For our new penitent, we pray to thee, Lord.
For your gift of this sacrament, we praise thee, Lord.

Lord, come into the depths of our souls and help us as a family to appreciate always the wonder of your forgiveness and to partake of your sacrament of penance regularly. Bless our child whose first confession is soon to take place. Erase his/her fears and fill him/her with the hope of your forgiving love.

A Confirmation Prayer

Come, Oh Holy Spirit, and fill the heart of our confirmand. Make him/her strong in purpose, pure in heart, and always Christian in motive.

Thank you for this son/daughter whom you blessed in baptism, blessed again in

First Communion and First Penance, and now bless in confirmation. Let the decision to be one of your chosen people fill him/her with joy, love, and your beloved Spirit.

On Death of a Parent and Grandparent

We have lost a dear parent and grandparent, Lord.

Be with us in our grief.

Let us remember both the life on earth he/she shared with us and the eternal happiness he/she now shares with you. You taught us, "He who believes in Me will have eternal life." Help us to remember that when the little memories that trigger our grief tug at us each day.

Thank you for this parent and grandparent, Lord—for the years of love and care, for the memories we shared, and for the hope you offer us.

First Funeral

Muffled voices
Silver box
Sacred sounds
Sweet scents
Words . . . tears . . .
Why?

Yes, suburban child
People die.
Why?

Sheltered from age, you
surrounded by youth, you
wonder . . .
God, can it be true
that someday
I . . . ?

Winning and Losing

Here she comes, Lord, and her disappointed face tells it all. She lost. Help me to find the right words to console her, to explain that in order to experience winning, we must also experience losing. Otherwise, how flat life's victories.

But when is it ever a good time to lose? Last time or next time, maybe, but never now. Should I remind her that she won the spelling bee in second grade? Or that she brought home four blue ribbons from fourth grade field day? Or that she was elected seventh grade senator? No, what good will that serve now? Later, perhaps. Now she needs to be consoled, to be told that even if she didn't get the lead, she has the better voice or that she would have gotten the lead if the director hadn't wanted to pass the roles around, giving everyone a chance. Help me to help her save face, Lord, while learning to accept wins and losses.

And while I'm at it, Lord, help me to accept losing, too. It hurts to see my children disappointed. Help me to realize that when my child loses, another child wins and that he deserves the joy of victory also.

Illness in the Family

Dearest Jesus, come into our family and make us well again. When one is ill, the rest of us also hurt. Grant wisdom to our doctors and nurses, patience to ourselves, and relief to our patients. You who healed the many while you walked on earth will not refuse to hear our prayer today.

For Children Going Away to College

Seek not grades but understanding.
Seek not popularity but friends.
Seek not promotion but fulfillment.
Seek not success but service.
Seek not pleasure but joy.
Seek not affluence but peace.
Seek not compromise but truth.
Seek not attention but respect.
Seek not yourself but others.
Seek not heaven but God.

An Engagement Prayer

Come into our home, Blessed Mother Mary, and share the joy of our engaged couple. Let their love radiate in our midst, engulfing us and renewing in us the joy of having others love us. Just as our Lord blessed you in your betrothal, bless our betrothed ones. Fill them with hope and let Christ become an integral part of their new life together.

Marriage

Lord, let not our marriage become stale and meaningless, a convenient shelter for married strangers.

Let us, rather, seek and find ever new joy and wonder in one another, reliving the excitement of our early discovery of love together. Help us to make you the foundation of our marriage, the nuptial Band that surrounds our love and keeps it sacred.

Wedding Anniversary

We praise and thank you for our years together —
for the joys and the sorrows
for the lean years and the full years
for the sons and the daughters
and all the rest.
We praise and thank you for bringing us together
and enriching that togetherness through you, and in
    you, and with you,
Oh Father, Son, and Holy Spirit.

Renewal of Wedding Vows

Husband: I, _____, again take you, _____, to be my wedded wife, to have and to hold from this day forward, for better or for worse, for richer or for poorer, in sickness and in health, until death do us part.

Wife: I, _____, again take you, _____, to be my wedded husband, to have and to hold from this day forward, for better or for worse, for richer or for poorer, in sickness and in health, until death do us part.

Together: May God continue to unite us in ever richer love and strengthen us for our lives ahead. May He fill our hearts with joy and our home with love. May He constantly remind us of His great gift of one another. May His blessings be upon our family forever.

Safe Travel

Oh, Good St. Joseph, patron saint of travellers, watch over our loved ones as they travel. Grant them safe planes, careful pilots, and good weather. Give them clear highways, reasonable speeds, and a concern for other drivers. Just as you guided Jesus and Mary safely back to Nazareth, return our loved ones to us safely.

Vacation Prayer in the Car with Tired Children

Oh, God of Peace,
invade our car and turn it into a haven of peace and
    quiet
for just a little while.
Give the children a little patience with one another
and us a lot more patience with them.
In the miles to go before we stop,
help them realize their power to make each other
    happy or unhappy.
Make them willing to share the windows,
to stop touching each other,
to stop asking when we'll get there.
Finally, dear Lord, teach us to appreciate
the luxury of auto travel today.
We could be travelling steerage across the Atlantic
or in a covered wagon across the Rockies.
Alongside such hazards, the kids' fighting seems
    insignificant.
Help us to hold our tempers for just a few more miles.

Graduation

Bless our graduate, Lord, and thank you for his/her education. Through the teachers, talents, and perseverence you sent, he/she has gained knowledge to face the future with hope. We pray that our graduate will use this education to your greater honor and glory, Lord, never forgetting a responsibility to those less learned.

And we also pray that we will all continue to be lifelong learners.

Halloween Prayer

Mother Mary, hallowed of hallowed
Come to my aid this hallowed season.
Give me inspiration, patience and Elmer's glue
to create something different
to hide my human goblins.
Ghosts and robots are out.
Cinderella is square
and who ever heard of Mickey Mouse?
Guide my needle true
and I pray, dear Mother,
to help me find time between
CCD and PTA
to watch for tricks
and buy the treats
and ponder once again
how this holiday all came about.

Thanksgiving

We thank Thee, Oh Lord God, giver of all fruits of the earth, for thy bounteous gifts: land, home, sustenance, and universe.

We thank Thee, Oh Lord God, creator of all that lives, for thy loving gifts: families, friends, communities, peoples.

We thank Thee, Oh Lord God, promiser of eternal life, for thy glorious gifts: your love, your Son, and your Holy Spirit.

10
Our Family Book of Life

We, _____ and _____ , freely chose one another in love and were married in God's grace at ____ o'clock on the ____ day of _____ in the year of ____ at _____ church in the city of _____ . Here follows a record of our life together thereon.

Births

Name _____ Date _____

Name _____ Date _____

Name _____ Date _____

Name _____ Date _____

Name _____ Date _____

Name _____ Date _____

Baptisms

Name _____ Date _____
Church _____
Godparents _____
Celebrant _____

Name _____ Date _____
Church _____
Godparents _____
Celebrant _____

Name _____ Date _____
Church _____
Godparents _____
Celebrant _____

Name _____ Date _____
Church _____
Godparents _____
Celebrant _____

Name _____ Date _____
Church _____
Godparents _____
Celebrant _____

First Communions

Name _____ Date _____

Place _____ Celebrant _____

Name _____ Date _____

Place _____ Celebrant _____

Name _____ Date _____

Place _____ Celebrant _____

Name _____ Date _____

Place _____ Celebrant _____

Name _____ Date _____

Place _____ Celebrant _____

Name _____ Date _____

Place _____ Celebrant _____

Name _____ Date _____

Place _____ Celebrant _____

Name _____ Date _____

Place _____ Celebrant _____

Confirmations

Name _____

Church _____

Sponsor_____Bishop _____

Name _____Date _____

Church _____

Sponsor_____Bishop _____

Name _____Date _____

Church _____

Sponsor_____Bishop _____

Patron Saints

Name _____Patron Saint_____
Feastday_____

Name _____Patron Saint_____
Feastday_____

Name _____Patron Saint_____
Feastday_____

Name _____Patron Saint_____
Feastday_____

Marriages

Names: _____and _____

Date _____Place_____

Celebrant _____

Names: _____and _____

Date _____Place_____

Celebrant _____

Names: _____and _____

Date _____Place_____

Celebrant _____

Names: _____and _____

Date _____Place_____

Celebrant _____

Names: _____and _____

Date _____Place_____

Celebrant _____

Religious Vocations

Name _____Date _____

Church_____Celebrant _____

Name _____Date _____

Church_____Celebrant _____

Deaths

Name _____Date _____

Age _____Cemetery _____

Celebrant_____

Name _____Date _____

Age _____Cemetery _____

Celebrant_____

Name _____Date _____

Age _____Cemetery _____

Celebrant_____

*Dear God, hold this family in the cup of your hand.
Watch over us with a loving eye. Keep us on your
path so that we may someday be joined together
again with you in heaven. Amen.*

Bibliography

Family Celebrations

Advent in Your Home; booklet; Larsen and Galvin; Liguorian Pamphlets and Books, Liguori, Mo.

Alleluia Days; Mary Louise Tietjen; Twenty-Third Publications; West Mystic, Ct.

And Then God Made Families; Dolores Curran; Alt-Curran Assoc., Inc.; Green Bay, Wi.

Bless the Lord! A Prayerbook for Advent, Christmas, Lent, and Eastertide; William G. Storey, ed.; Ave Maria Press; Notre Dame, Ind.

Celebrate Summer! A Guidebook for Families; Elizabeth Jeep and Gabe Huck; Paulist Press, New York.

Celebrating Advent; Bob Heyer, ed.; booklet; New Catholic World; Paulist Press, New York.

Celebrating: Family Prayer Services; Marey Hopkins, O.P. ed.; Paulist Press, New York.

Celebrations for Children: Fred Thompson; Cookbook approach offering guidance to every phase of organization and planning; Twenty-Third Publications, West Mystic, Ct.

Children's Liturgies: Seventy-four Eucharistic liturgies, prayer services, and penance services designed for primary, middle, and junior high children; Bernadette Kenny, R.S.H.M.; Paulist Press; New York.

Children's Liturgies; Virginia Sloyan and Gabe Huck, eds.; The Liturgical Conference, Washington, D.C.

Children of Joy: Raising Your Own Home-Grown Christians; a parents' guide to the first dozen years; David and Elizabeth Gray; Readers Press Inc., Branford, Ct.

Come, Be Reconciled: Youth Penance Resources; Hall, Rabalais, Vavasseur; Paulist Press, New York.

Come Out! Blandford, Bucher, Blunt and Miffleton, World Library Publications, World Library of Sacred Music, 2145 Central Pkway, Cincinnati, Oh.

Communion: Between Parent, Teacher and Child; McIntyre, Twenty-Third Publications; West Mystic, CT.

Everything You Need for Children's Worship (Except

131

Children); Jack Noble White; St. Anthony Messenger Press; Cincinnati, Ohio.

Experimental Liturgy Book; Hoey; Seabury Press; New York.

Family, A religious education program; Sr. Maureen Gallagher; Paulist Press, New York.

Family Celebrations for Religious Education; filmstrip; Dolores Curran; Twenty-Third Publications; W. Mystic, CT.

Family Nights, Lent and Easter: Terry and Mimi Reilly; Abbey Press; St. Meinrad, Ind.

Hassle: Dealing with Family Relationships; Lyman Coleman; Creative Resources; Waco, Tex.

Hi God! Kinghorn and Landry; North American Liturgy Resources, Cincinnati, Ohio.

Home: Resources for Family Sharing; Office of Religious Education, Dubuque, Iowa.

How Green is Green? LeBranc and Talbot; Ave Maria Press, Notre Dame, Ind.

It's All in the Family; filmstrip; Dolores Curran; Twenty-Third Publications; West Mystic, CT.

Lectionary for Children's Mass; Aldo J. Tos, ed.; Pueblo Publishing Co.; New York.

Liturgies for Children; Andrew Jamison; St. Anthony Messenger Press; Cincinnati, Ohio.

Major Feasts and Seasons; Vol. One, Number One, "Advent" and Vol. One Number Two, "Lent"; The Liturgical Conference, Washington, D.C.

My Beginning Mass Book; JoAnn Marie Angers; Simplified Mass prayers for children; Twenty-Third Publications, West Mystic, CT.

My Nameday, Come for Dessert; McLoughlin; Liturgical Press; Collegeville, Mn.

Parishes and Families; Huck and Sloyan, eds.; The Liturgical Conference; Washington, D.C.

The Passover Meal; A Ritual for Christian Homes; Arleen Hynes; Paulist Press, New York.

Rediscovering Lent Through Prayer and Ministry; Magazine; *Today's Parish;* February, 1978; Twenty-Third Publications; W. Mystic, CT.

See His Banners Go; Marxhausen; Concordia Publishing House; St. Louis, Mo.

Signs, Songs and Stories: Another Look at Children's Liturgies; Sloyan; The Liturgical Conference, Inc.; Washington, D.C.

This Is the Word of the Lord; 34 Liturgies of the Word for Holy Week, major feasts and selected Sundays arranged in dialogue form for three readers; William J. Freburger, ed.; Ave Maria Press; Notre Dame, Ind.

Touching God; Thomas and Nieland, Ave Maria Press, Notre Dame, Ind.

We Talk with God: Devotions for Family and Group Use; Lucille E. Hein; Fortress Press; Philadelphia, Pa.

What Do You Say to a Child When You Meet a Flower? O'Neill; Abbey Press; St. Meinrad, Ind.

Who, Me Teach My Child Religion? Dolores Curran; Winston Press, Minneapolis, Mn.

Meditation

Comtemplative Prayer, Problems and an Approach for the Ordinary Christian; Rev. Alan J. Placa; Living Flame Press; Locust Valley, New York.

Hope for the Flowers; Trina Paulus; Paulist Press; New York.

How to Meditate: A Guide to Self-Discovery; Lawrence LeShan; Bantam Books, New York.

Listening for the Lord: Sr. Gloriana Bednarski, RSM; Twenty-Third Publications, West Mystic, CT.

A Hunger for Wholeness; Joan Hutson; Ave Maria Press; Notre Dame, Ind.

Kitchen Table Christianity; Isaias Powers, C.P.; St. Anthony Messenger Press; Cincinnati, Ohio.

On the Run; Spirituality for the Seventies; Michael McCauley; St. Thomas More Assoc., Chicago.

Petals of Prayer; Creative Ways to Pray; Rev. Paul Sauve; Living Flame Press; Locust Valley, New York.

Prayer Is a Hunger; Edward J. Farrell; Dimension Books, Denville, N.J.

Quiet Places with Jesus; Isaias Powers, C.P.; Twenty-Third Publications, West Mystic, CT.

Prayer

Day by Day: The Notre Dame Prayerbook for Students; Thomas McNally and William Storey, eds.; Ave Maria Press; Notre Dame, Ind.

Every Day and All Day; St. Anthony Messenger Book of Prayers, New and Old; Leonard Foley, O.F.M. ed.; St. Anthony Messenger Press, Cincinnati, Oh.

Faith, Hope, Love, Joy, Prayer; A Book of Prayers by the Handicapped for the Handicapped; booklet; Apostolate to the Handicapped; Box 2221, Madison, Wi.

Family Retreat Program; Mary Reardon and Sr. Susanne Lachapelle, RSM; Twenty-Third Publications, West Mystic, CT.

He Touched Me; My Pilgrimage of Prayer; John Powell, S.J.; Argus Communications; Niles, Ill.

How to Have Family Prayers; Rosalind Rinker; Zondervan Pub. House, Grand Rapids, Mi.

How to Pray Today; A Book of Spiritual Reflections; Yves Raguin, S.J.; Abbey Press; St. Meinrad, Ind.

I've Got to Talk to Somebody, God; Marjorie Holmes; Doubleday; Garden City, New York.

Lift Up My Spirit, Lord! Medard Laz; Emmaus Books, Paulist Press, New York.

Lord, Be With; Herbert Brokering; Concordia Pub. House; St. Louis.

My Beginning Prayer Book; Sr. Regina Torzewski, O.L.V.M.; First prayers for children; Twenty-Third Publications, West Mystic, CT.

Praise Him! A Prayerbook for Today's Christian; William G. Storey, ed.; Ave Maria Press; Notre Dame, Ind.

Pray; Step by Step Directions and Guidance for Praying; Richard J. Huelsman, S.J.; Paulist Press, New York.

Prayer: Family Style; The Commission on the Liturgy; Green Bay, Wi.

Prayer in the Shower; Benjamin T. Mackin, O.Praem; The Commission on the Liturgy; Green Bay, Wi.

Prayer Without Frills; Juan Arias; Abbey Press; St. Meinrad, Ind. 47577.

Prayers for All Times; booklet; Donald C. Campbell, ed.; The Paulist League, New York.

Prayers from a Mother's Heart; Judith Mattison; Augsburg Pub. House; Minneapolis.

Song of the Sparrow; Meditations and Poems to Pray By; Murray Bodo; St. Anthony Messenger Press; Cincinnati, Oh.

Steps into Light; A Prayerbook of Christian Belief; Rev. James W. Lyons; Ave Maria Press; Notre Dame, Ind.

Who Am I, God? The Doubts, the fears, the joys of being a woman; Marjorie Holmes; Doubleday; Garden City, New York.

Saints

Elizabeth Ann Seton, Wife, Mother, Sister, Saint; A Biography for Young Readers; Janet S. Wiley; St. Anthony Messenger Press, Cincinnati, Ohio.

Once-Upon-a-Time Saints; Faith-Tales for Children; Ethel Marbach; St. Anthony Messenger Press, Cincinnati, Ohio.

Saint of the Day; two volumes; Leonard Foley, O.F.M.; St. Anthony Messenger Press; Cincinnati, Ohio.

Saints for Confused Times; John Garvey; St. Thomas More Press; Chicago.

The Saints in Season; Austin Flannery, O.P., ed.; Liturgical Press; Collegeville, Mn.

Saints in Times of Turmoil; John V. Sheridan; Paulist Press; New York.

Scripture

Arch Books; Bible Stories in verse or prose; Concordia Pub. House, St. Louis.

Bible Heroes; Ruth Shannon Odor; Standard Publishing; Cincinnati, Ohio.

A Bible Prayer-Book for Today; Peter DeRosa; Fountain Books, Cleveland, Ohio.

Bible Stories, Retold; David Kossoff; Follett Publishing Co.; Chicago.

Children's Bible; Golden Press, New York.

Children Bible; Lawrence Atkinson; Liturgical Press; Collegeville, Mn.

The Children's New Testament; Gleason Ledyard, Trans.; Word Books, Waco, Texas.

Good News for Modern Man; The New Testament in Today's English Version; American Bible Society.

I Find My Joy in the Lord; Roger J. Radley, ed.; from the Grail translation of the Psalms; Emmaus Books; Paulist Press; New York.

The Jerusalem Bible; Alexander Jones, ed.; Doubleday, New York.

The New American Bible; Members of the Catholic Biblical Association of America; P.J. Kennedy & Sons; New York.

Psalms for Beginners; The Liturgical Press; Collegeville, Mn.

The Psalms for Modern Man; American Bible Society.

Purple Puzzle Tree; bible stories for children; Concordia Pub. House, St. Louis, Mo.

The Taize Picture Bible; adapted from the Jerusalem Bible; Fortress Press, Philadelphia, Pa.

The Way; Bible paraphrased for youth; Tyndale House Publishers; Wheaton, Ill.

Way of the Cross

Everyman's Way of the Cross; Clarence Enzler; Ave Maria Press, Notre Dame, Ind.

The Way of the Cross; A Traditional Devotion for Personal or Group Prayer with Contemporary Meditations; William V. Coleman; Twenty-Third Publications; West Mystic, CT.

The Way of the Cross; traditional pamphlet; The Liturgical Press; Collegeville, Mn.

The Way of the Cross for Children; Harfmann and Holly; Barton-Cotton, Inc.; Baltimore.

The Way of the Cross Today for Children; Charles E. Jones; Ave Maria Press; Notre Dame, Ind.

Addresses of Publishers of Materials Mentioned in This Book

Note to Readers: I found that many families do not have access to religious bookstores or secular bookstores large enough to stock a wide variety of religious books. Yet, obtaining some of the books I mentioned is important to many of the rituals and experiences I suggested.

There are three ways of obtaining these books and materials. Attend your diocesan religious education congress if you can. All of the major publishers have booths or exhibits with a wide variety of their books for sale. Secondly, ask your diocesan office of religious education or even your director of religious education in your parish to help you obtain certain books. They have catalogs and addresses and sometimes know where a book can be purchased locally.

Thirdly, write to the publisher at the address below and ask him if it is available in your area. If so, where? If not, please send it and bill you. Since trying to find publisher's addresses can discourage the most confirmed celebrator, here is a directory of them for your convenience.

Abbey Press
St. Meinrad, In. 47577

Alt-Curran Assoc., Inc.
300 Dauphin St.
Green Bay, Wi. 54301

American Bible Society
1865 Broadway
New York, N.Y. 10023

Argus Communications
7440 Natchez Ave.
Niles, Il. 60648

Augsburg Publishing House
426 S. Fifth St.
Minneapolis, Mn. 55415

Ave Maria Press
Notre Dame, In. 46556

Bantam Books, Inc.
666 Fifth Ave.
New York, N.Y. 10019

Barton-Cotton, Inc.
1405 Parker Rd.
Baltimore, Md. 21227

Concordia Publishing House
3558 S. Jefferson Avenue
St. Louis, Mo. 63118

Creative Resources
Box 1790
Waco, Texas 76703

Dimension Books, Inc.
P.O. Box 811
Denville, N.J. 07834

Doubleday & Co., Inc.
245 Park Ave.
New York, N.Y. 10017

Dubuque, Archdiocese of
Office of Religious Ed.
1229 Mount Loretta
Dubuque, Ia. 52001

Follett Pub. Co.
1010 Washington Blvd.
Chicago, Il. 60607

Fortress Press
2900 Queen Lane
Philadelphia, Pa. 19129

Fountain Books
Collins, William and World
Pub. Co., Inc.

2080 W. 117th St.
Cleveland, Oh. 44111

Green Bay Dept. of Ed.
Box 186
Green Bay, Wi. 54305

Liguori Publications
Liguori, Mo. 63057

The Liturgical Conference
1221 Mass. Ave., N.W.
Washington, D.C. 20005

Liturgical Press
St. John's Abbey
Collegeville, Mn. 56321

Living Flame Press
P.O. Box 74
Locust Valley, N.Y. 11560

Paulist Press
545 Island Road
Ramsey, New Jersey
07446

Pueblo Publishing Co.
1860 Broadway
New York, N.Y. 10023

Readers Press, Inc.
Branford, Ct.

Seabury Press, Inc.
815 Second Ave.
New York, N.Y. 10017

St. Anthony Messenger
Press
1615 Republic St.
Cincinnati, Oh. 45210

The Thomas More
Association
180 N. Wabash Ave.
Chicago, Il. 60601

Twenty-Third
Publications
P.O. Box 180
West Mystic, Ct. 06388

Tyndale House Publishers
Box 80
Wheaton, Ill. 60187

Winston Press
430 Oak Grove
Minneapolis, Mn. 55403

Word Books, Inc.
4800 W. Waco Dr.
Waco, Tx. 76703

World Library Publications, Inc.
2145 Central Parkway
Cincinnati, Oh. 45214

Zondervan Publishing House
1415 Lake Dr., S.E.
Grand Rapids, Mi. 49506

Index